Learn Software Testing in

By Krishna Rungta

Table Of Content

Section 1: Introduction
1. What is Software Testing? Why is it Important?
2. 7 Software Testing Principles
3. What is V Model
4. Software Testing Life Cycle - STLC explained
5. Test Plan
6. What is Manual testing?
7. What is Automation Testing?

Section 2: Creating Test
1. What is Test Scenario?
2. How to Write Test Case
3. How to Create Requirements Traceability Matrix
4. Boundary Value Analysis & Equivalence Partitioning
5. Static Testing
6. Test Environment
7. Test Data
8. What is Defect?
9. Defect Life Cycle

Section 3: Testing Types

1. 100+ Types of Software Testing
2. Unit Testing
3. INTEGRATION Testing

4. System Testing
5. Regression Testing
6. Sanity Testing & Smoke Testing
7. Performance Testing
8. Load Testing
9. Accessibility Testing
10. STRESS Testing
11. User Acceptance Testing
12. Backend Testing
13. Protocol Testing
14. Scrum Testing Beginners
15. Web Service Testing

Section 4: Testing Different Domains
1. Banking Domain Application Testing
2. Ecommerce Applications
3. Insurance Application Testing
4. Payment Gateway Testing
5. Retail POS Testing
6. Telecom Domain Testing

Section 1: Introduction

What is Software Testing? Why is it Important?

What is Software Testing?

Software testing is an activity to check whether the actual results match the expected results and to ensure that the software system is defect free. It involves execution of a software component or system component to evaluate one or more properties of interest.

Software testing also helps to identify errors, gaps or missing requirements in contrary to the actual requirements. It can be either done manually or using automated tools. Some prefer saying Software testing as a white box and black box testing.

This tutorial introduces testing software to the audience and justifies its importance

Please be patient. The Video will load in some time. If you still face issue viewing video click here

Why is Software Testing Important?

Testing is important because software bugs could be expensive or even dangerous. Software bugs can potentially cause monetary and human loss, history is full of such examples.

- In April 2015, Bloomberg terminal in London crashed due to software glitch affected more than 300,000 traders on financial markets. It forced the government to postpone a 3bn pound debt sale.

- Nissan cars have to recall over 1 million cars from the market due to software failure in the airbag sensory detectors. There has been reported two accident due to this software failure.

- Starbucks was forced to close about 60 percent of stores in the U.S and Canada due to software failure in its POS system. At one point store served coffee for free as they unable to process the transaction.

- Some of the Amazon's third party retailers saw their product price is reduced to 1p due to a software glitch. They were left with heavy losses.

- Vulnerability in Window 10. This bug enables users to escape from security sandboxes through a flaw in the win32k system.

- In 2015 fighter plane F-35 fell victim to a software bug, making it unable to detect targets correctly.

- China Airlines Airbus A300 crashed due to a software bug on April 26, 1994, killing 264 innocent live

- In 1985, Canada's Therac-25 radiation therapy machine malfunctioned due to software bug and delivered lethal radiation doses to patients, leaving 3 people dead and critically injuring 3 others.

- In April of 1999, a software bug caused the failure of a $1.2 billion military satellite launch, the costliest accident in history

- In may of 1996, a software bug caused the bank accounts of 823 customers of a major U.S. bank to be credited with 920 million US dollars.

Types of Software Testing

Typically Testing is classified into three categories.

- Functional Testing

- Non-Functional Testing or Performance Testing

- Maintenance (Regression and Maintenance)

Testing Category	Types of Testing
Functional Testing	<ul><li>Unit Testing</li><li>Integration Testing</li></ul>

	• Smoke
	• UAT (User Acceptance Testing)
	• Localization
	• Globalization
	• Interoperability
	• ⍰ So on
Non-Functional Testing	• Performance
	• Endurance
	• Load
	• Volume
	• Scalability
	• Usability
	• ⍰ So on
Maintenance	• Regression
	• ⍰ Maintenance

This is not the complete list as there are more than **150 types of testing** types and still adding. Also, note that not all testing types are applicable to all projects but depend on nature & scope of the project.

7 Software Testing Principles

Here are the 7 Principles:
1) Exhaustive testing is not possible

Yes!Exhaustive testing is not possible. Instead, we need the optimal amount of testing based on the risk assessment of the application.

And the million dollar question is, how do you determine this risk ?

To answer this let's do an exercise

In your opinion, Which operation is most likely to cause your Operating system to fail?

I am sure most of you would have guessed, Opening 10 different application all at the same time.

So if you were testing this Operating system, you would realize that defects are likely to be found in multi-tasking activity and need to be tested thoroughly which brings us to our next principle Defect Clustering

2) Defect Clustering

Defect Clustering which states that a small number of modules contain most of the defects detected. This is the application of the Pareto Principle to software testing: approximately 80% of the problems are found in 20% of the modules.

By experience, you can identify such risky modules. But this approach has its own problems

If the same tests are repeated over and over again , eventually the same test cases will no longer find new bugs.

3) Pesticide Paradox

Repetitive use of the same pesticide mix to eradicate insects during farming will over time lead to the insects developing resistance to the pesticide Thereby ineffective of pesticides on insects. The same applies to software testing. If the same set of repetitive tests are conducted, the method will be useless for discovering new defects.

To overcome this, the test cases need to be regularly reviewed & revised , adding new & different test cases to help find more defects.

Testers cannot simply depend on existing test techniques. He must look out continually to improve the existing methods to make testing more effective. But even after all this sweat & hard work in testing, you can never claim your product is bug free. To drive home this point , let's see this video of public launch of Windows 98

You think a company like MICROSOFT would not have tested their OS thoroughly & would risk their reputation just to see their OS crashing during its public launch!

4) Testing shows presence of defects

Hence, testing principle states that - Testing talks about the presence of defects and don't talk about the absence of defects. i.e. Software Testing reduces the probability of undiscovered defects remaining in the software but even if no defects are found, it is not a proof of correctness.

But what if , you work extra hard , taking all precautions & make your software product 99% bug-free. And the software does not meet the needs & requirements of the clients.

This leads us to our next principle, which states that- Absence of Error

5) Absence of Error

It is possible that software which is 99% bug-free is still unusable. This can be the case if the system is tested thoroughly for the wrong requirement. Software testing is not mere finding defects, but also to check that software addresses the business needs. Absence of Error is a Fallacy i.e. Finding and fixing defects does not help if the system build is unusable and does not fulfill the user's needs & requirements.

To solve this problem , the next principle of testing states that Early Testing

6) Early Testing

Early Testing - Testing should start as early as possible in the Software Development Life Cycle. So that any defects in the requirements or design phase are captured in early stages. It is much cheaper to fix a defect in early stages of testing. But how early one should start testing? It is recommended that you start finding the bug the moment the requirements are defined. More on this principle in a later training tutorial.

7) Testing is context dependent

Testing is context dependent which basically means that the way you test an e-commerce site will be different from the way you test a commercial off the shelf application. All the developed software's are not identical. You might use a different approach, methodologies, techniques and types of testing depending upon the application type. For instance testing, any POS system at a retail store will be different than testing an ATM machine.

Summary of the Seven Testing Principles

Principle 1	Testing shows presence of defects
Principle 2	Exhaustive testing is impossible
Principle 3	Early Testing
Principle 4	Defect Clustering
Principle 5	Pesticide Paradox
Principle 6	Testing is context dependent
Principle 7	Absence of errors - fallacy

Myth: "Principles are just for reference. I will not use them in practise."

This is so very untrue. Test Principles will help you create an effective test strategy and draft error catching test cases.

But learning testing principles is just like learning to drive for the first time.

Initially while you learn to drive, you pay attention to each and everything like gear shifts, speed, clutch handling, etc. But with experience, you just focus on driving the rest comes naturally. Such that you even hold conversations with other passengers in the car.

Same is true for testing principles. Experienced testers have internalized these principles to a level that they apply them even without thinking. Hence the myth that the principles are not use in practise is simply not true.

What is V Model

This tutorial explains in detail the Software/System Development Life Cycle (SDLC) like the **Waterfall cycle & Iterative cycle like RAID & Agile**. And further, it proceeds to explain the V-Model of testing and STLC (Software Test Life Cycle).

Suppose, you are assigned a task, to develop a custom software for a client. Now, irrespective of your technical background, try and make an educated guess about the sequence of steps you will follow, to achieve the task.

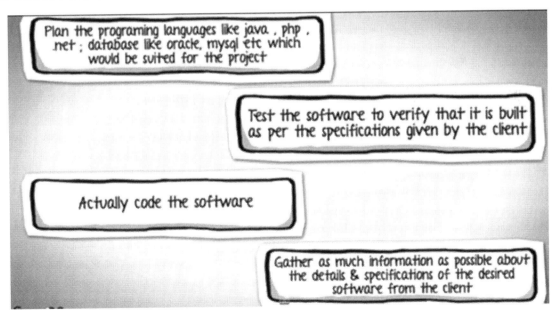

The correct sequence would be.

Different phases of Software Development	Activities performed in each stage

Cycle	
Requirement Gathering stage	• Gather as much information as possible about the details & specifications of the desired software from the client. This is nothing but the Requirements gathering stage.
Design Stage	• Plan the programming language like **Java**, **PHP**, .net; database like Oracle, MySQL, etc. Which would be suited for the project, also some high-level functions & architecture.
Built Stage	• After design stage, it is built stage, that is nothing but actually code the software
Test Stage	• Next, you test the software to verify that it is built as per the specifications given by the client.
Deployment stage	• Deploy the application in the respective environment
Maintenance stage	• Once your system is ready to use, you may require to change the code later on as per customer request

All these levels constitute the **waterfall method** of software development lifecycle. As you may observe, that **testing in the model starts only after implementation is done**.

But if you are working in the large project, where the systems are complex, it's easy to miss out the key details in the requirements phase itself. In such cases, an entirely wrong product will be delivered to the client and you might have to start afresh with the project OR if you manage to note the requirements correctly but make serious mistakes in design and architecture of your software you will have to redesign the entire software to correct the error.

Assessments of thousands of projects have shown that **defects introduced during requirements & design make up close to half of the total number of defects.**

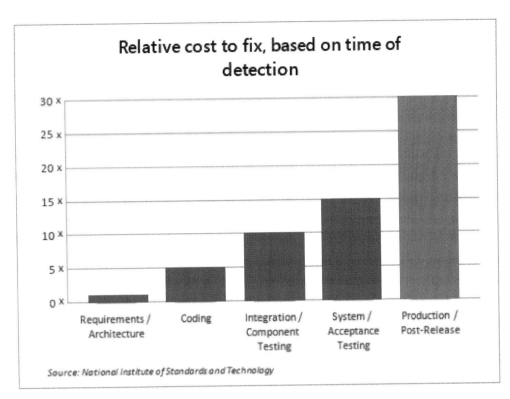

Relative cost to fix, based on time of detection

Source: National Institute of Standards and Technology

Also, the **costs of fixing a defect increases across the development life cycle. The earlier in life cycle a defect is detected, the cheaper it is to fix it.** As the say, "A stitch in time saves a nine."

To address this concern, **the V model of testing** was developed where **for every phase, in the Development life cycle there is a corresponding Testing phase**

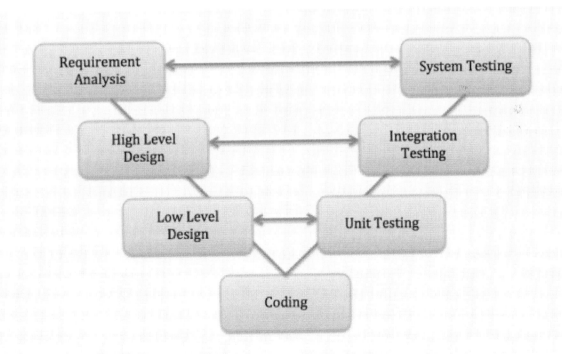

- The left side of the model is Software Development Life Cycle - **SDLC**

- The right side of the model is Software Test Life Cycle - **STLC**

- The entire figure looks like a V, hence the name **V - model**

Apart from V model, there are iterative development models, where development is carried in phases, with each phase adding a functionality to the software. Each phase comprises of its independent set of development and testing activities.

Good examples of Development lifecycles following iterative method are Rapid Application Development, Agile Development

Here are the Key Terms again:

- **SDLC:**

  SDLC is Software Development Life Cycle. It is the sequence of activities carried out by Developers to design and develop high-quality software.

  Though SDLC uses the term 'Development', it does not involve just coding tasks done by developers but also incorporates the tasks contributed by testers and stakeholders.

  In SDLC, test cases are created.

- **STLC:**

  STLC is Software Testing Life Cycle. It consists of series of activities carried out by Testers methodologically to test your software product.

  Though STLC uses the term "testing" it does not involve just testers, at some instances, they have to involve developers as well.

  In STLC Test cases are executed.

- **Waterfall Model:**

  Waterfall model is a sequential model divided into different phases of software development activity. Each stage is designed for performing specific activity during SDLC phase. Testing phase in waterfall model starts only after implementation of the system is done.

  Testing is done within the SDLC.

- **V- Model:**

  V- model is an extension of the waterfall model. Unlike waterfall model, In V-model, there is a corresponding testing phase for each software development phase. Testing in V-model is done in parallel to SDLC stage.

  Testing is done as a sub project of SDLC.

Conclusion

There are numerous development life cycle models. **Development model selected for a project depends on the aims and goals of that project.**

- Testing is not a stand-alone activity, and it has to adapt the development model chosen for the project.

- In any model, testing should performed at all levels i.e. right from requirements until maintenance.

Software Testing Life Cycle - STLC explained

What is Software Testing Life Cycle (STLC)?

Software Testing Life Cycle (STLC) is defined as a sequence of activities conducted to perform Software Testing.

It consists of series of activities carried out methodologically to help certify your software product.

Diagram - Different stages in Software Test Life Cycle

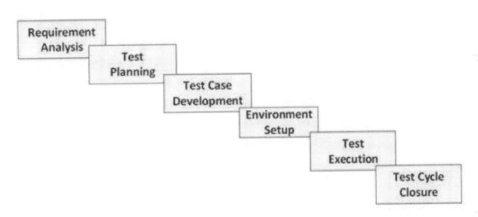

Each of these stages have a definite Entry and Exit criteria; , Activities & Deliverables associated with it.

What is Entry and Exit Criteria?

Entry Criteria: Entry Criteria gives the prerequisite items that must be completed before testing can begin.

Exit Criteria: Exit Criteria defines the items that must be completed before testing can be concluded

You have Entry and Exit Criteria for all levels in the Software Testing Life Cycle (STLC)

In an Ideal world you will not enter the next stage until the exit criteria for the previous stage is met. But practically this is not always possible. So for this tutorial, we will focus on activities and deliverables for the different stages in STLC life cycle. Lets look into them in detail.

Requirement Analysis

During this phase, test team studies the requirements from a testing point of view to identify the testable requirements.

The QA team may interact with various stakeholders (Client, Business Analyst, Technical Leads, System Architects etc) to understand the requirements in detail.

Requirements could be either Functional (defining what the software must do) or Non Functional (defining system performance /security availability)

.Automation feasibility for the given testing project is also done in this stage. **Activities**

- Identify types of tests to be performed.

- Gather details about testing priorities and focus.

- Prepare **Requirement Traceability Matrix (RTM)**.

- Identify test environment details where testing is supposed to be carried out.

- Automation feasibility analysis (if required).

Deliverables

- RTM

- Automation feasibility report. (if applicable)

Test Planning

This phase is also called **Test Strategy** phase. Typically , in this stage, a Senior QA manager will determine effort and cost estimates for the project and would prepare and finalize the Test Plan. **Activities**

- Preparation of test plan/strategy document for various types of testing

- Test tool selection

- Test effort estimation

- Resource planning and determining roles and responsibilities.

- Training requirement

Deliverables

- **Test plan** /strategy document.

- **Effort estimation** document.

Test Case Development

This phase involves creation, verification and rework of test cases & test scripts. **Test data** , is identified/created and is reviewed and then reworked as well.

Activities

- Create test cases, automation scripts (if applicable)

- Review and baseline test cases and scripts

- Create test data (If Test Environment is available)

Deliverables

- Test cases/scripts

- Test data

Test Environment Setup

Test environment decides the software and hardware conditions under which a work product is tested. Test environment set-up is one of the critical aspects of testing process and **_can be done in parallel with Test Case Development Stage_**. **_Test team may not be involved in this activity_** if the customer/development team provides the test environment in which case the test team is required to do a readiness check (smoke testing) of the given environment. **Activities**

- Understand the required architecture, environment set-up and prepare hardware and software requirement list for the Test Environment.

- Setup test Environment and test data

- Perform smoke test on the build

Deliverables

- Environment ready with test data set up

- Smoke Test Results.

Test Execution

During this phase test team will carry out the testing based on the test plans and the test cases prepared. Bugs will be reported back to the development team for correction and retesting will be performed. **Activities**

- Execute tests as per plan

- Document test results, and log defects for failed cases

- Map defects to test cases in RTM

- Retest the defect fixes

- Track the defects to closure

Deliverables

- Completed RTM with execution status

- Test cases updated with results

- Defect reports

Test Cycle Closure

Testing team will meet , discuss and analyze testing artifacts to identify strategies that have to be implemented in future, taking lessons from the current test cycle. The idea is to remove the process bottlenecks for future test cycles and share best practices for any similar projects in future. **Activities**

- Evaluate cycle completion criteria based on Time,Test coverage,Cost,Software,Critical Business Objectives , Quality

- Prepare test metrics based on the above parameters.

- Document the learning out of the project

- Prepare Test closure report

- Qualitative and quantitative reporting of quality of the work product to the customer.

- Test result analysis to find out the defect distribution by type and severity.

Deliverables

- Test Closure report

- Test metrics

Finally, *summary* of STLC Phases along with Entry and Exit Criteria

STLC Stage	Entry Criteria	Activity	Exit Criteria	Deliverables
Requirement Analysis	Requirements Document available (both functional and non functional) Acceptance criteria defined. Application architectural document available.	Analyse business functionality to know the business modules and module specific functionalities. Identify all transactions in the modules. Identify all the user profiles. Gather user interface/authentication, geographic spread requirements. Identify types of tests to be performed.	Signed off RTM Test automation feasibility report signed off by the client	RTM Automation feasibility report (if applicable)

		Gather details about testing priorities and focus. Prepare Requirement Traceability Matrix (RTM). Identify test environment details where testing is supposed to be carried out. Automation feasibility analysis (if required).		
Test Planning	Requirements Documents Requirement Traceability matrix. Test automation feasibility document.	Analyze various testing approaches available Finalize on the best suited approach Preparation of test plan/strategy document for various types of testing Test tool selection Test effort estimation Resource planning and determining roles and responsibilities.	Approved test plan/strategy document. Effort estimation document signed off.	Test plan/strategy document. Effort estimation document.
Test case development	Requirements Documents RTM and test plan Automation analysis report	Create test cases, automation scripts (where applicable) Review and baseline test cases and scripts Create test data	Reviewed and signed test Cases/scripts Reviewed and signed test data	Test cases/scripts Test data

Test Environment setup	System Design and architecture documents are available Environment set-up plan is available	Understand the required architecture, environment set-up Prepare hardware and software requirement list Finalize connectivity requirements Prepare environment setup checklist Setup test Environment and test data Perform smoke test on the build Accept/reject the build depending on smoke test result	Environment setup is working as per the plan and checklist Test data setup is complete Smoke test is successful	Environment ready with test data set up Smoke Test Results.
Test Execution	Baselined RTM, Test Plan , Test case/scripts are available Test environment is ready Test data set up is done Unit/Integration test report for the build to be tested is available	Execute tests as per plan Document test results, and log defects for failed cases Update test plans/test cases, if necessary Map defects to test cases in RTM Retest the defect fixes Regression testing of application Track the defects to closure	All tests planned are executed Defects logged and tracked to closure	Completed RTM with execution status Test cases updated with results Defect reports

Test Cycle closure	Testing has been completed Test results are available Defect logs are available	Evaluate cycle completion criteria based on - Time, Test coverage , Cost , Software Quality , Critical Business Objectives Prepare test metrics based on the above parameters. Document the learning out of the project Prepare Test closure report Qualitative and quantitative reporting of quality of the work product to the customer. Test result analysis to find out the defect distribution by type and severity	Test Closure report signed off by client	Test Closure report Test metrics

Test Plan

What is a Test Plan?

A test plan is a detailed document that outlines the test strategy, **Testing** objectives, resources (manpower, software, hardware) required for testing, test schedule, test estimation and test deliverables.

The test plan serves as a blueprint to conduct software testing activities as a defined process which is minutely monitored and controlled by the test manager.

Let's start with following scenario

In a meeting, you want to discuss the Test Plan with the team members, but they are not interested

In such case, what will you do? Select your answer as following figure

Importance of Test Plan

Making Test Plan has multiple benefits

- Test Plan helps us determine the **effort** needed to validate the quality of the application under test

- Help people outside the test team such as developers, business managers, customers **understand** the details of testing.

- Test Plan **guides** our thinking. It is like a rule book, which needs to be followed.

- Important aspects like test estimation, test scope, test strategy are **documented** in Test Plan, so it can be reviewed by Management Team and re-used for other projects.

How to write a Test Plan

You already know that making a **Test Plan** is the most important task of Test Management Process. Follow the seven steps below to create a test plan as per IEEE 829

1. Analyze the product

2. Design the Test Strategy

3. Define Test Criteria

4. Define the Test Objectives

5. Resource Planning

6. Plan Test Environment

7. Schedule & Estimation

8. Determine Test Deliverables

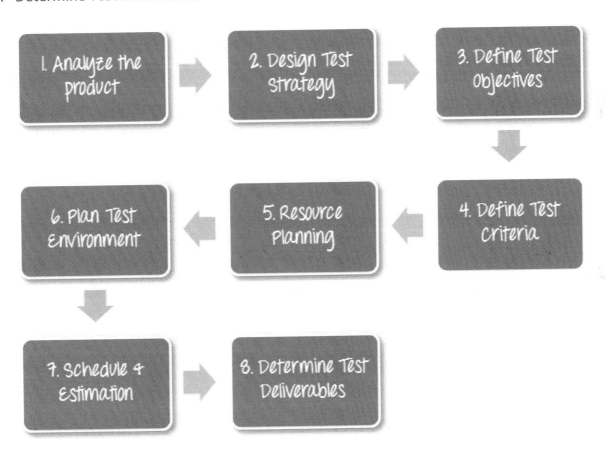

Step 1) Analyze the product

How can you test a product **without** any information about it? The answer is **Impossible.** You must learn a product **thoroughly** before testing it.

The product under test is Guru99 banking website. You should research clients and the end users to know their needs and expectations from the application

- Who will use the website?

- What is it used for?

- How will it work?

- What are software/ hardware the product uses?

You can use the following approach to analyze the site

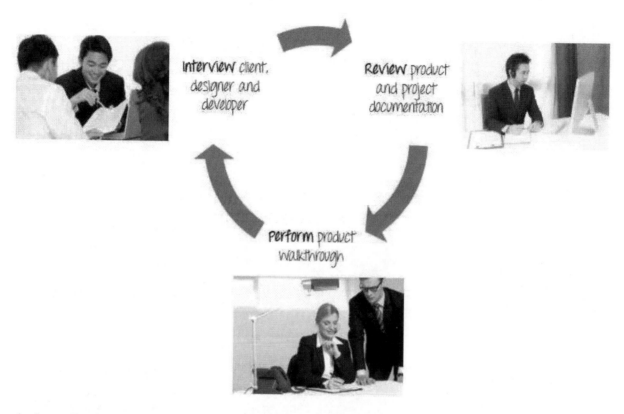

Now let's apply above knowledge to a real product: **Analyze** the banking
website **http://demo.guru99.com/V4**.

You should take a **look around** this website and also **review product documentation**. Review of
product documentation helps you to understand all the features of the website as well as how to
use it. If you are unclear on any items, you might **interview** customer, developer, designer to get
more information.

Step 2) Develop Test Strategy

Test Strategy is a **critical step** in making a Test Plan. A Test Strategy document, is a high-level document, which is usually developed by Test Manager. This document defines:

- The project's **testing objectives** and the means to achieve them

- Determines testing **effort** and **costs**

Back to your project, you need to develop Test Strategy for testing that banking website. You should follow steps below

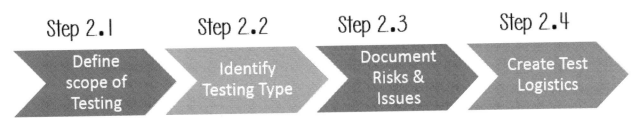

Step 2.1) Define Scope of Testing

Before the start of any test activity, scope of the testing should be known. You must think hard about it.

- The components of the system to be tested (hardware, software, middleware, etc.) are defined as "**in scope**"

- The components of the system that will not be tested also need to be clearly defined as being "**out of scope.**"

Defining the scope of your testing project is very important for all stakeholders. A precise scope helps you

- Give everyone a **confidence & accurate information** of the testing you are doing

- All project members will have a **clear** understanding about what is tested and what is not

HOW DO YOU DETERMINE SCOPE YOUR PROJECT?

To determine scope, you must –

- Precise customer requirement

- Project Budget

- Product Specification

- Skills & talent of your test team

Now should clearly define the "in scope" and "out of scope" of the testing.

- As the software requirement **specs**, the project Guru99 Bank only focus on testing all the **functions** and external interface of website **Guru99** Bank (**in scope** testing)

- Nonfunctional testing such as **stress**, **performance** or **logical database** currently will not be tested. (**out of** scope)

Problem Scenario

The customer wants you to test his API. But the project budget does not permit to do so. In such a case what will you do?

Well, in such case you need to convince the customer that API testing is extra work and will consume significant resources. Give him data supporting your facts. Tell him if API testing is included in-scope the budget will increase by XYZ amount.

The customer agrees and accordingly the new scopes, out of scope items are

- In-scope items: Functional Testing, API Testing

- Out of scope items: Database testing, hardware & any other external interfaces

Step 2.2) Identify Testing Type

A **Testing Type** is a standard test procedure that gives an expected test outcome.

Each testing type is formulated to identify a specific type of product bugs. But, all Testing Types are aimed at achieving one common goal "**Early detection of** all the defects before releasing the product to the customer"

The **commonly used** testing types are described as following figure

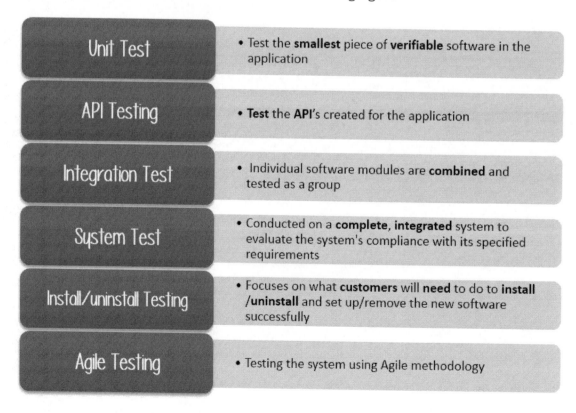

Unit Test	• Test the **smallest** piece of **verifiable** software in the application
API Testing	• **Test** the **API**'s created for the application
Integration Test	• Individual software modules are **combined** and tested as a group
System Test	• Conducted on a **complete, integrated** system to evaluate the system's compliance with its specified requirements
Install/uninstall Testing	• Focuses on what **customers** will **need** to do to **install /uninstall** and set up/remove the new software successfully
Agile Testing	• Testing the system using Agile methodology

There are **tons of Testing Types** for testing software product. Your team **cannot have** enough efforts to handle all kind of testing. As Test Manager, you must set **priority** of the Testing Types

- Which Testing Types should be **focused** for web application testing?

- Which Testing Types should be **ignored** for saving Cost

- Risk is future's **uncertain event** with a probability of **occurrence** and a **potential** for loss. When the risk actually happens, it becomes the '**issue'.**

In the article **Risk Analysis and Solution**, you have already learned about the 'Risk' analysis in detail and identified potential risks in the project.

In the Test Plan, you will document those risks

Risk	Mitigation
Team member lack the required skills for website testing.	Plan **training course** to skill up your members
The project schedule is too tight; it's hard to complete this project on time	Set **Test Priority** for each of the test activity.
Test Manager has poor management skill	Plan **leadership training** for manager
A lack of cooperation negatively affects your employees' productivity	**Encourage** each team member in his task, **and inspire** them to greater efforts.
Wrong budget estimate and cost overruns	Establish the **scope** before beginning work, pay a lot of attention to project planning and constantly track and measure the progress

Step 2.4) Create Test Logistics

In Test Logistics, the Test Manager should answer the following questions:

- **Who** will test?

- **When** will the test occur?

Who will test?

You may not know exact names of the tester who will test, but the **type of tester** can be defined.

To select the right member for specified task, you have to consider if his skill is qualified for the task or not, also estimate the project budget. Selecting wrong member for the task may cause the project to **fail** or **delay**.

Person having the following skills is most ideal for performing software testing:

- Ability to **understand** customers point of view

- Strong **desire** for quality

- **Attention** to detail

- Good **cooperation**

In your project, the member who will take in charge for the test execution is the **tester.** Base on the project budget, you can choose in-source or outsource member as the tester.

When will the test occur?

Test activities must be matched with associated development activities.

You will start to test when you have **all required items** shown in following figure

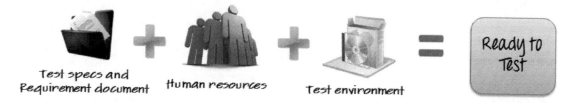

Test specs and Requirement document   Human resources   Test environment   Ready to Test

Step 3) Define Test Objective

Test Objective is the overall goal and achievement of the test execution. The objective of the testing is finding as many software defects as possible; ensure that the software under test is **bug free** before release.

To define the test objectives, you should do 2 following steps

1. List all the software features (functionality, performance, GUI...) which may need to test.

2. Define the **target** or the **goal** of the test based on above features

Let's apply these steps to find the test objective of your Guru99 Bank testing project

You can choose the **'TOP-DOWN'** method to find the website's features which may need to test. In this method, you break down the application under test to **component** and **sub-component**.

In the previous topic, you have already analyzed the requirement specs and walk through the website, so you can create a **Mind-Map** to find the website features as following

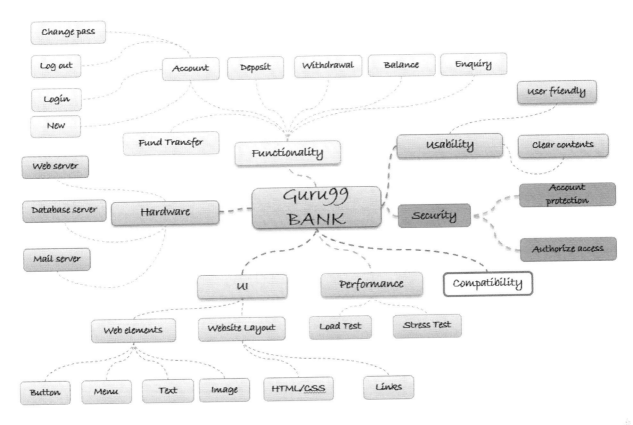

This figure shows all the features which the Guru99 website may have.

Based on above features, you can define the Test Objective of the project Guru99 as following

- Check that whether website Guru99 **functionality**(Account, Deposit...) is working as expected without any error or bugs in real business environment

- Check that the external interface of the website such as **UI** is working as expected and & meet the customer need

- Verify the **usability** of the website. Are those functionalities convenient for user or not?

Step 4) Define Test Criteria

Test Criteria is a standard or rule on which a test procedure or test judgment can be based. There're 2 types of test criteria as following

Suspension Criteria

Specify the critical suspension criteria for a test. If the suspension criteria are met during testing, the active test cycle will be **suspended** until the criteria are **resolved**.

Example: If your team members report that there are **40%** of test cases failed, you should **suspend** testing until the development team fixes all the failed cases.

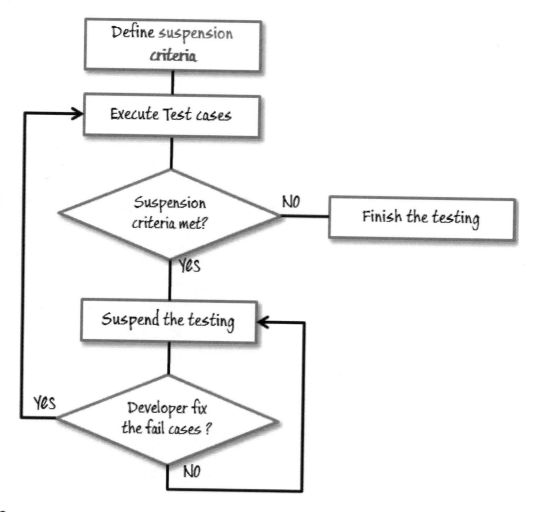

Exit Criteria

It specifies the criteria that denote a **successful** completion of a test phase. The exit criteria are the targeted results of the test and are necessary before proceeding to the next phase of development. Example: **95%** of all critical test cases must pass.

Some methods of defining exit criteria are by specifying a targeted **run rate** and **pass rate**.

- Run rate is ratio between **number test cases executed/total test cases** of test specification. For example, the test specification has total 120 TCs, but the tester only executed 100 TCs, So the run rate is 100/120 = 0.83 (83%)

- Pass rate is ratio between **numbers test cases passed / test cases executed**. For example, in above 100 TCs executed, there're 80 TCs that passed, so the pass rate is 80/100 = 0.8 (80%)

This data can be retrieved in Test Metric documents.

- **Run** rate is mandatory to be **100%** unless a clear reason is given.

- **Pass** rate is dependent on project scope, but **achieving high pass rate** is a goal.

Example: Your Team has already done the test executions. They report the test result to you, and they want you to confirm the **Exit Criteria**.

In above case, the Run rate is mandatory is **100%,** but the test team only completed 90% of test cases. It means the Run rate is not satisfied, so do NOT confirm the Exit Criteria

Step 5) Resource Planning

Resource plan is a **detailed summary** of all types of resources required to complete project task. Resource could be human, equipment and materials needed to complete a project

The resource planning is important factor of the test planning because helps in **determining** the **number** of resources (employee, equipment...) to be used for the project. Therefore, the Test Manager can make the correct schedule & estimation for the project.

This section represents the recommended resources for your project.

Human Resource

The following table represents various members in your project team

No.	Member	Tasks
1.	Test Manager	**Manage** the whole project Define project **directions** Acquire appropriate resources
2.	Tester	Identifying and describing appropriate test techniques/tools/automation architecture

		Verify and assess the Test Approach
		Execute the tests, **Log** results, **Report** the defects.
		Tester could be in-sourced or out-sourced members, base on the project budget
		For the task which required **low** skill, I recommend you choose **outsourced** members to **save** project cost.
3.	Developer in Test	**Implement**the test cases, test program, test suite etc.
4.	Test Administrator	Builds up and ensures test environment and assets are **managed** and **maintained**
		SupportTester to use the test environment for test execution
5.	SQA members	Take in charge of quality assurance
		Check to confirm whether the testing process is meeting specified requirements

System Resource

For testing, a web application, you should plan the resources as following tables:

No.	Resources	Descriptions
1.	Server	Install the web application under test
		This includes a separate web server, database server, and application server if applicable
2.	Test tool	The testing tool is to automate the testing, simulate the user operation, generate the test results
		There are tons of test tools you can use for this project such as Selenium, QTP...etc.
3.	Network	You need a Network include LAN and Internet to simulate the real business and user environment
4.	Computer	The PC which users often use to connect the web server

Step 6) Plan Test Environment
What is the Test Environment

A testing environment is a setup of software and hardware on which the testing team is going to execute test cases. The test environment consists of **real business** and **user** environment, as well as physical environments, such as server, front end running environment.

How to setup the Test Environment

Back to your project, how do you set up **test environment** for this banking website?

To finish this task, you need **a strong cooperation** between Test Team and Development Team

You should ask the developer some questions to understand the web application under test **clearly**. Here're some recommended questions. Of course, you can ask the other questions if you need.

- What is the maximum user connection which this website can handle at the same time?

- What are hardware/software requirements to install this website?

- Does the user's computer need any particular setting to browse the website?

Following figure describes the test environment of the banking website **www.demo.guru99.com/V4**

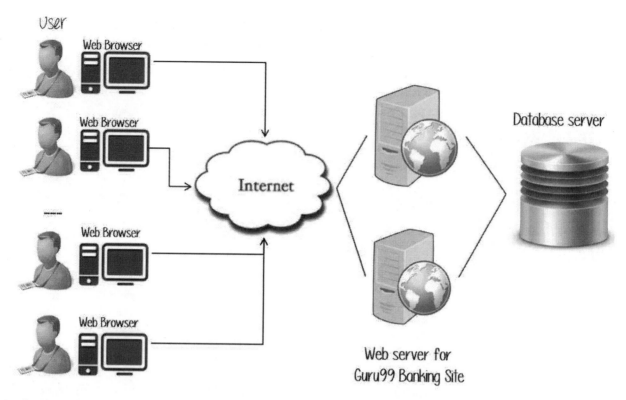

Step 7) Schedule & Estimation

In the article **Test estimation**, you already used some techniques to estimate the effort to complete the project. Now you should include that estimation as well as the schedule to the Test Planning

In the Test Estimation phase, suppose you break out the whole project into small tasks and add the estimation for each task as below

Task	Members	Estimate effort
Create the test specification	Test Designer	170 man-hour
Perform Test Execution	Tester, Test Administrator	80 man-hour
Test Report	Tester	10 man-hour
Test Delivery		20 man-hour
Total		**280 man-hour**

Then you create the **schedule** to complete these tasks.

Making schedule is a common term in project management. By creating a solid schedule in the Test Planning, the Test Manager can use it as tool for monitoring the project progress, control the cost overruns.

To create the project schedule, the Test Manager needs several types of input as below:

- **Employee and project deadline**: The working days, the project deadline, resource availability are the factors which affected to the schedule

- **Project estimation**: Base on the estimation, the Test Manager knows how long it takes to complete the project. So he can make the appropriate project schedule

- **Project Risk** : Understanding the risk helps Test Manager add enough extra time to the project schedule to deal with the risks

Let's practice with an example:

Suppose the boss wants to complete the project Guru99 in **one** month, you already estimated the effort for each tasks in Test Estimation. You can create the schedule as below

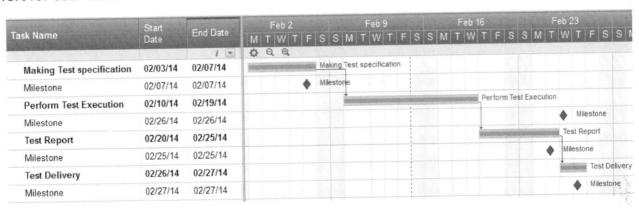

Step 8) Test Deliverables

Test Deliverables is a list of all the documents, tools and other components that has to be developed and maintained in support of the testing effort.

There are different test deliverables at every phase of the software development lifecycle.

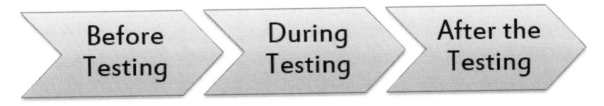

Test deliverables are provided **before** testing phase.

- Test plans document.

- Test cases documents

- Test Design specifications.

Test deliverables are provided **during** the testing

- Test Scripts

- Simulators.

- Test Data

- Test Traceability Matrix

- Error logs and execution logs.

Test deliverables are provided **after** the testing cycles is over.

- **Test Results/reports**

- Defect Report

- Installation/ Test procedures guidelines

- **Release notes**

· **What is Manual testing?**

What is Manual testing?

Manual Testing is a type of Software Testing where Testers manually execute test cases without using any automation tools.

Manual testing is the most primitive of all testing types and helps find bugs in the software system.

Any new application must be manually tested before its testing can be automated. Manual testing requires more effort, but is necessary to check automation feasibility.

Manual Testing does not require knowledge of any testing tool.

One of the Software Testing Fundamental is "**100% Automation is not possible**".

This makes Manual Testing imperative.

Types of Manual Testing :

Below given diagram depicts Manual Testing Types. In fact any type of software testing type can be executed both manually as well using an automation tool.

Myths of Manual Testing

Following are few common myths and facts related to testing:

Myth: Anyone can do manual testing

Fact: Testing requires many skill sets

Myth: Testing ensures 100% defect free product

Fact: Testing attempts to find as many defects as possible. Identifying all possible defects is impossible.

Myth: Automated testing is more powerful than manual testing

Fact: 100% test automation cannot be done. Manual Testing is also essential.

Myth: Testing is easy

Fact: Testing can be extremely challenging .Testing an application for possible use cases with minimum test cases requires high analytical skills.

Manual Testing vs Automation Testing

Manual Testing	Automated Testing
Manual testing requires human intervention for test execution.	Automation Testing is use of tools to execute test cases
Manual testing will require skilled labour, long time & will imply high costs.	Automation Testing saves time, cost and manpower. Once recorded, it's easier to run an automated test suite
Any type of application can be tested manually, certain testing types like ad-hoc and monkey testing are more suited for manual execution.	Automated testing is recommended only for stable systems and is mostly used for regression testing
Manual testing can be become repetitive and boring.	The boring part of executing same test cases time and again, is handled by automation software in automation testing.

Tools to Automate Manual Testing

- **Selenium**
- **QTP**
- **Jmeter**
- **Loadrunner**

- **TestLink**

- **Quality Center(ALM)**

Conclusion

Manual testing is an activity where the tester needs to be very patient, creative & open minded.

They need to think and act with an End User perspective.

What is Automation Testing?

Manual testing is performed by a human sitting in front of a computer carefully executing the test steps.

Automation Testing means using an automation tool to execute your test case suite.

The automation software can also enter test data into the System Under Test , compare expected and actual results and generate detailed test reports.

Test Automation demands considerable investments of money and resources.

Successive development cycles will require execution of same test suite repeatedly.

Using a test automation tool it's possible to record this test suite and re-play it as required.

Once the test suite is automated, no human intervention is required .

This improved ROI of Test Automation.

Goal of Automation is to reduce number of test cases to be run manually and not eliminate manual testing all together.

Why Automated Testing?

Automated software testing is important due to following reasons:

- Manual Testing of all work flows, all fields , all negative scenarios is time and cost consuming

- It is difficult to test for multi lingual sites manually

- Automation does not require Human intervention. You can run automated test unattended (overnight)

- Automation increases speed of test execution

- Automation helps increase Test Coverage

- Manual Testing can become boring and hence error prone.

Which Test Cases to Automate?

Test cases to be automated can be selected using the following criterion to increase the automation ROI

- High Risk - Business Critical test cases

- Test cases that are executed repeatedly

- Test Cases that are very tedious or difficult to perform manually

- Test Cases which are time consuming

The following category of test cases are not suitable for automation:

- Test Cases that are newly designed and not executed manually atleast once

- Test Cases for which the requirements are changing frequently

- Test cases which are executed on ad-hoc basis.

Automated Testing Process:

Following steps are followed in an Automation Process

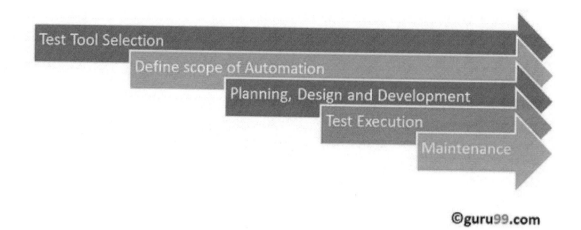

Test tool selection

Test Tool selection largely depends on the technology the Application Under Test is built on. For instance **QTP** does not support Informatica. So QTP cannot be used for testing **Informatica** applications. **It's a good idea to conduct Proof of Concept of Tool on AUT**

Define the scope of Automation

Scope of automation is the area of your Application Under Test which will be automated. Following points help determine scope:

- Feature that are important for the business

- Scenarios which have **large amount of data**

- **Common functionalities** across applications

- Technical feasibility

- Extent to which business components are reused

- **Complexity** of test cases

- Ability to use the same test cases for cross browser testing

Planning, Design and Development

During this phase you create Automation strategy & plan, which contains following details-

- Automation tools selected

- Framework design and its features

- In-Scope and Out-of-scope items of automation

- Automation test bed preparation

- Schedule and Timeline of scripting and execution

- Deliverables of automation testing

Test Execution

Automation Scripts are executed during this phase. The scripts need input test data before there are set to run. Once executed they provide detailed test reports.

Execution can be performed using the automation tool directly or through the Test Management tool which will invoke the automation tool.

Example: Quality center is the Test Management tool which in turn it will invoke QTP for execution of automation scripts. Scripts can be executed in a single machine or a group of machines. The execution can be done during night , to save time.

Maintenance

 As new functionalities are added to the System Under Test with successive cycles, Automation Scripts need to be added, reviewed and maintained for each release cycle. **Maintenance becomes necessary to improve effectiveness of Automation Scripts.**

Framework in Automation

A framework is set of automation guidelines which help in

- Maintaining consistency of Testing

- Improves test structuring

- Minimum usage of code

- Less Maintenance of code

- Improve re-usability

- Non Technical testers can be involved in code

- Training period of using the tool can be reduced

- Involves Data wherever appropriate

There are four types of framework used in automation software testing:

1. Data Driven Automation Framework

2. Keyword Driven Automation Framework

3. Modular Automation Framework

Hybrid Automation Framework

Automation Tool Best Practices

To get maximum ROI of automation, observe the following

- Scope of Automation needs to be determined in detail before the start of the project. This sets expectations from Automation right.

- Select the right automation tool: A tool must not be selected based on its popularity but it's fit to the automation requirements.

- Choose appropriate framework

- Scripting Standards- Standards have to be followed while writing the scripts for Automation .Some of them are-

    - Create uniform scripts, comments and indentation of the code

    - Adequate Exception handling - How error is handled on system failure or unexpected behavior of the application.

    - User defined messages should be coded or standardized for Error Logging for testers to understand.

- Measure metrics- Success of automation cannot be determined by comparing the manual effort with the automation effort but by also capturing the following metrics.

    - Percent of defects found

    - Time required for automation testing for each and every release cycle

    - Minimal Time taken for release

    - Customer satisfaction Index

    - Productivity improvement

The above guidelines if observed can greatly help in making your automation successful.

Benefits of Automation Testing

Following are benefits of automated testing:

- 70% faster than the manual testing

- Wider test coverage of application features

- Reliable in results

- Ensure Consistency

- Saves Time and Cost

- Improves accuracy

- Human Intervention is not required while execution

- Increases Efficiency

- Better speed in executing tests

- Re-usable test scripts

- Test Frequently and thoroughly

- More cycle of execution can be achieved through automation

- Early time to market

Different types of software testing that can be automated

- Smoke Testing

- Unit Testing

- Integration Testing

- Functional Testing

- Keyword Testing

- Regression Testing

- Data Driven Testing

- Black Box Testing

How to Choose an Automation Tool?

Selecting the right tool can be a tricky task. Following criterion will help you select the best tool for your requirement-

- Environment Support

- Ease of use

- Testing of Database

- Object identification

- Image Testing

- Error Recovery Testing

- Object Mapping

- Scripting Language Used

- Support for various types of test - including functional, test management, mobile, etc...

- Support for multiple testing frameworks

- Easy to debug the automation software scripts

- Ability to recognize objects in any environment

- Extensive test reports and results

- Minimize training cost of selected tools

Tool selection is one of biggest challenges to be tackled before going for automation. First, Identify the requirements, explore various tools and its capabilities, set the expectation from the tool and go for a Proof Of Concept.

Automation Testing Tools

There are tons of Functional and Regression Testing Tools available in market. Here are 5 best tools certified by our experts

Selenium

It is a software testing tool used for regression testing. It is an open source testing tool that provides playback and recording facility for regression testing. The **Selenium** IDE only supports Mozilla Firebox web browser.

- It provides the provision to export recorded script in other languages like Java, Ruby, RSpec, Python, C#, **Junit** and TestNG

- It can execute multiple tests at a time

- Autocomplete for Selenium commands that are common

- Walkthrough tests

- Identifies the element using id, name , X-path, etc.

- Store tests as Ruby Script, HTML, and any other format

- It provides an option to assert the title for every page

- It supports selenium user-extensions.js file
- It allows to insert comments in the middle of the script for better understanding and debugging

QTP (HP UFT)

It is widely used for functional and regression testing, it addresses every major software application and environment. To simplify test creation and maintenance, it uses the concept of keyword driven testing. It allows the tester to build test cases directly from the application.

- It is easier to use for non-technical person to adapt to and create working test cases
- It fix defects faster by thoroughly documenting and replicating defects for developer
- Collapse test creation and test documentation at a single site
- Parameterization is easy than WinRunner
- QTP supports .NET development environment
- It has better object identification mechanism
- It can enhance existing QTP scripts without "Application Under Test" being available, by using the ActiveScreen

Rational Functional Tester

It is an Object-Oriented automated functional testing tool that is capable of performing automated functional, regression, data-driven testing and GUI testing. The main features of this tool are

- It supports a wide range of protocols and applications like Java, HTML, NET, Windows, SAP, Visual basic, etc.
- It can record and replay the actions on demand
- It integrates well with source control management tools such as Rational Clear Case and Rational Team Concert integration
- It allows developers to create keyword associated script so that it can be re-use
- Eclipse **Java** Developer Toolkit editor facilitates the team to code test scripts in Java with Eclipse
- It supports custom controls through proxy SDK (Java/.Net)
- It supports version control to enable parallel development of test scripts and concurrent usage by geographically distributed team

WATIR

It is an open source testing software for regression testing. It enables you to write tests that are easy to read and maintain. Watir supports only internet explorer on windows while Watir webdriver supports Chrome, Firefox, IE, Opera, etc.

- It supports multiple browsers on different platforms

- Rather than using proprietary vendorscript it uses a full featured modern scripting language Ruby

- It supports your web app regardless of what it is developed in

SilkTest

Silk Test is designed for doing functional and regression testing. For e-business application, silk test is the leading functional testing product. It is a product of Segue Software takeover by Borland in 2006. It is an object oriented language just like C++. It uses the concept of object, classes, and inheritance. Its main feature includes

- It consists of all the source script files

- It converts the script commands into GUI commands. On the same machine, commands can be run on a remote or host machine

- To identify the movement of mouse along with keystrokes, Silktest can be executed. It can avail both playback and record method or descriptive programming methods to get the dialogs

- It identifies all controls and windows of the application under test as objects and determine all of the attributes and properties of each window

Section 2: Creating Test

What is Test Scenario?

What is a Test Scenario?

A Test Scenario is any functionality that can be tested. It is also called **Test Condition or Test Possibility**. As a tester, you may put yourself in the end user's shoes and figure out the real-world scenarios and use cases of the Application Under Test.

What is Scenario Testing?

Scenario Testing is a variant of Software Testing where Scenarios are Used for Testing. Scenarios help in an Easier Way of Testing of the more complicated Systems

Let's study this with the help of the video below -

Why create Test Scenarios?

Test Scenarios are created for following reasons,

- Creating Test Scenarios ensures complete Test Coverage

- Test Scenarios can be approved by various stakeholders like Business Analyst, Developers, Customers to ensure the Application Under Test is thoroughly tested. It ensures that the software is working for the most common use cases.

- They serve as a quick tool to determine the testing work effort and accordingly create a proposal for the client or organize the workforce.

- They help determine the most important end-to-end transactions or the real use of the software applications.

- For studying the end-to-end functioning of the program, Test Scenario is critical.

When not create Test Scenario?

Test Scenarios may not be created when

- The Application Under Test is complicated, unstable and there is a time crunch in the project.

- Projects that follow Agile Methodology like Scrum, Kanban may not create Test Scenarios.

- Test Scenario may not be created for a new bug fix or regression testing. In such cases, Test Scenarios must be already heavily documented in the previous test cycles. This is especially true for Maintenance projects.

How to create a Test Scenario

As a tester, you can follow these five steps to create Test Scenarios-

- **Step 1**: Read the Requirement Documents like BRS, SRS, FRS, of the System Under Test (SUT). You could also refer uses cases, books, manual, etc. of the application to be tested.

- **Step 2**: For each requirement, figure out possible users actions and objectives. Determine the technical aspects of the requirement. Ascertain possible scenarios of system abuse and evaluate users with hacker's mindset.

- **Step 3:** After reading the Requirements Document and doing your due Analysis, list out different test scenarios that verify each feature of the software.

- **Step 4:** Once you have listed all possible Test Scenarios, a Traceability Matrix is created to verify that each & every requirement has a corresponding Test Scenario

- **Step 5:** The scenarios created are reviewed by your supervisor. Later, they are also reviewed by other Stakeholders in the project.

Tips to Create Test Scenarios

- Each Test Scenario should be tied to a minimum of one Requirement or User Story as per the Project Methodology.

- Before creating a Test Scenario that verifies multiple Requirements at once, ensure you have a test scenario that checks that requirement in isolation.

- Avoid creating overly complicated Test Scenarios spanning multiple Requirements.

- The number of scenarios may be large, and it is expensive to run them all. Based on customer priorities only run selected Test Scenarios

Example 1: Test Scenario for Flight Reservation

For the Flight Reservation Application, a few test scenarios would be

Test Scenario 1: Check the Login Functionality

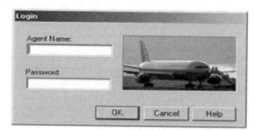

Test Scenario 2: Check that a New Order can be created

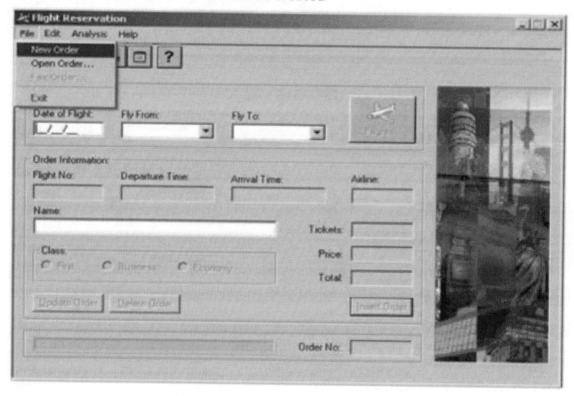

Test Scenario 3: Check that an existing Order can be opened

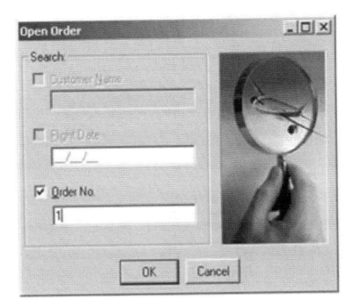

Test Scenario 4: Check that a user, can FAX an order

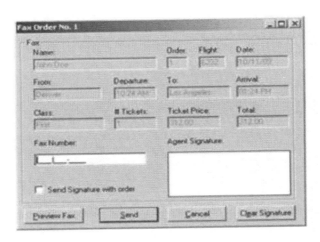

Test Scenario 5: Check that the information displayed in the HELP section is correct

Test Scenario 6: Check that the information displayed in About section, like version, programmer name, copy right information is correct

Apart from these six scenarios here is the list of all other scenarios

- Update Order

- Delete Order

- Check Reports

- Check Graphs and so on.

Next, we have already learned **exhaustive testing is not possible**. Suppose you have time only to execute 4 out of these 6 scenarios which two low priority scenarios of these six will you eliminate. Think, your time starts now

I am sure most of you would have guessed scenarios 5 & 6 since they are not the core functionality of the application. This is nothing but **Test Prioritization**.

Example 2: Test Scenarios for a Banking Site

Test Scenario 1: Check the Login and Authentication Functionality

Test Scenario 2: Check Money Transfer can be done

Test Scenario 3: Check Account Statement can be viewed

Test Scenario 4: Check Fixed Deposit/Recurring Deposit can be created

And so on...

How to Write Test Case

What is Test Case?

A Test Case is a set of actions executed to verify a particular feature or functionality of your software application.

This tutorial describes test case designing and the importance of its various components.

Now, consider the Test Scenario Check Login Functionality there many possible cases like

Test Case 1: Check results on entering valid User Id & Password

Test Case 2: Check results on entering Invalid User ID & Password

Test Case 3: Check response when User ID is Empty & Login Button is pressed, and many more

This is nothing but Test Case. Test scenarios are rather vague and cover a wide range of possibilities. Testing is all about being very specific.Hence, we need Test Cases

Format of Standard Test Cases

Below is format of a standard login Test case

Test Case ID	Test Scenario	Test Steps	Test Data	Expected Results	Actual Results	Pass/Fail
TU01	Check Customer Login with valid Data	1. Go to site **http://demo.guru99.com** 2. Enter UserId 3. Enter Password 4. Click Submit	Userid = guru99 Password = pass99	User should Login into application	As Expected	Pass
TU02	Check Customer Login with invalid	1. Go to site **http://demo.guru99.com** 2. Enter UserId	Userid = guru99 Password = glass99	User should not Login into application	As Expected	Pass

Data	3. Enter Password
	4. Click Submit

While drafting a test case do include the following information

- The description of what requirement is being tested

- The explanation of how the system will be tested

- The test setup like: version of application under test, software, data files, operating system, hardware, security access, physical or logical date, time of day, prerequisites such as other tests and any other setup information pertinent to the requirements being tested

- Inputs and outputs or actions and expected results

- Any proofs or attachments

- Use active case language

- Test Case should not be more than 15 steps

- Automated test script is commented with inputs, purpose and expected results

- Setup offers alternative to pre-requisite tests

- With other tests, it should be incorrect business scenario order

Best Practice for writing good Test Case Example.

1. Test Cases need to be simple and transparent:

Create test cases that are as simple as possible. They must be clear and concise as the author of test case may not execute them.

Use assertive language like go to home page, enter data, click on this and so on. This makes the understanding the test steps easy and test execution faster.

2. Create Test Case with End User in Mind

Ultimate goal of any software project is to create test cases that meets customer requirements and is easy to use and operate. A tester must create test cases keeping in mind the end user perspective

3. Avoid test case repetition.

Do not repeat test cases. If a test case is needed for executing some other test case, call the test case by its test case id in the pre-condition column

4. Do not Assume

Do not assume functionality and features of your software application while preparing test case. Stick to the Specification Documents.

5. Ensure 100% Coverage

Make sure you write test cases to check all software requirements mentioned in the specification document. Use Traceability Matrix to ensure no functions/conditions is left untested.

6. Test Cases must be identifiable.

Name the test case id such that they are identified easily while tracking defects or identifying a software requirement at a later stage.

7. Implement Testing Techniques

It's not possible to check every possible condition in your software application. Testing techniques help you select a few test cases with the maximum possibility of finding a defect.

Boundary Value Analysis (BVA): As the name suggests it's the technique that defines the testing of boundaries for specified range of values.

Equivalence Partition (EP): This technique partitions the range into equal parts/groups that tend to have the same behavior.

State Transition Technique: This method is used when software behavior changes from one state to another following particular action.

Error Guessing Technique: This is guessing/anticipating the error that may arise while testing. This is not a formal method and takes advantages of a tester's experience with the application

8. Self cleaning

The test case you create must return the test environment to the pre-test state and should not render the test environment unusable. This is especially true for configuration testing.

9. Repeatable and self-standing

The test case should generate the same results every time no matter who tests it

10. Peer Review.

After creating test cases, get them reviewed by your colleagues. Your peers can uncover defects in your test case design, which you may easily miss.

Test Case Management Tools

Test management tools are the automation tools that help to manage and maintain the Test Cases. Main Features of a test case management tool are

1. **For documenting Test Cases:** With tools you can expedite Test Case creation with use of templates

2. **Execute the Test Case and Record the results:** Test Case can be executed through the tools and results obtained can be easily recorded.

3. **Automate the Defect Tracking:** Failed tests are automatically linked to the bug tracker , which in turn can be assigned to the developers and can be tracked by email notifications.

4. **Traceability:** Requirements, Test cases, Execution of Test cases are all interlinked through the tools, and each case can be traced to each other to check test coverage.

5. **Protecting Test Cases:** Test cases should be reusable and should be protected from being lost or corrupted due to poor version control. Test Case Management Tools offer features like

   - Naming and numbering conventions

   - Versioning

   - Read only storage

   - Controlled access

   - Off-site backup

Popular Test Management tools are : **Quality Center** and **JIR**20170809**A**

How to Create Requirements Traceability Matrix

What is Traceability Matrix?(RTM)

A traceability matrix is a document that co-relates any two-baseline documents that require a many-to-many relationship to check the completeness of the relationship.

It is used to track the requirements and to check the current project requirements are met.

What is RTM (Requirement Traceability Matrix)?

Requirement Traceability Matrix or RTM captures all requirements proposed by the client or development team and their traceability in a single document delivered at the conclusion of the life-cycle.

In other words, it is a document that maps and traces user requirement with test cases. The main purpose of Requirement Traceability Matrix is to see that all test cases are covered so that no functionality should miss while testing.

Requirement Traceability Matrix – Parameters include

- Requirement ID

- Risks

- Requirement Type and Description

- Trace to design specification

- Unit test cases

- Integration test cases

- System test cases

- User acceptance test cases

- Trace to test script

Types of Traceability Test Matrix

- **Forward traceability**: This matrix is used to check whether the project progresses in the desired direction and for the right product. It makes sure that each requirement is applied to the product and that each requirement is tested thoroughly. It maps requirements to test cases.

- **Backward or reverse traceability:** It is used to ensure whether the current product remains on the right track. The purpose behind this type of traceability is to verify that we are not expanding the scope of the project by adding code, design elements, test or other work that is not specified in the requirements. It maps test cases to requirements.

- **Bi-directional traceability (Forward+Backward):** This traceability metrics ensures that all requirements are covered by test cases. It analyzes the impact of a change in requirements affected by the defect in a work product and vice versa.

How to create Requirement Traceability Matrix

Let's understand the concept of Requirement Traceability Matrix through a Guru99 banking project.

On the basis of **Business Requirement Document (BRD)** and **Technical Requirement Document (TRD)**, testers start writing test cases.

Let suppose, the following table is our Business Requirement Document or **BRD** for **Guru99 banking project**.

Here the scenario is that the customer should be able to login to Guru99 banking website with the correct password and user#id while manager should be able to login to the website through customer login page.

BR#	Module Name	Applicable Roles	Description
B1	Login and Logout	Manager Customer	**Customer:** A customer can login using the login page **Manager:** A manager can login using the login page f customer. Post Login homepage will show ifferent links based on role
B2	Enquiry	Customer	ustomer: A customer can have multiple bank accounts. He can view balance of his accounts only **Manager:** A manager can view balance of all the customers who come under his supervision
B3	Fund Transfer	Manager Customer	**Customer:** A customer can have transfer funds from his "own" account to any destination account. **Manager:** A manager can transfer funds from any

Business Requirement # for Guru99 banking project

While the below table is our **Technical Requirement Document (TRD)**.

Login

> **T92** User-ID must not be blank
>
> **T93** Password must not be blank|
>
> **T94** If userid and password are valid. Login

Here is our TRD (Technical Requirement Document)

Note: QA teams do not document the BRD and TRD. Also some companies use **Function Requirement Documents (FRD)** which are similar to Technical Requirement Document but the process of creating traceability matrix remains the same.

Let's Go Ahead and create RTM Testing

Step 1: Our Test Case is

"Verify Login, when correct ID and Password is entered, it should login successfully"

TestCase #	Test Case	Test Steps	Test Data	Expected Result
1	Verify Login	1) Go to Login Page 2) Enter UserID 3) Enter Password 4) Click Login	id= Guru99 pass= 1234	Login Successful

When correct password and id entered, it should login successfully

Step 2: Identify the Technical Requirement that this test case is verifying. For our test case, the technical requirement is T94 is being verified.

T94   If userid and password are valid. Login

> T94 is our technical requirement that verifies successful login

Step 3: Note this Technical Requirement (T94) in the Test Case.

TestCase #	TR #	Note the Technical Requirement in the test case	Test Steps	Test Data	Expected
1	T94	Verify Login	1) Go to Login Page 2) Enter UserID 3) Enter Password 4) Click Login	id= Guru99 pass= 1234	Login Successful

Step 4: Identify the Business Requirement for which this TR (Technical Requirement-T94) is defined

BR#	Module Name	Applicable Roles	Description
B1	Login and Logout	Manager Customer	**Customer:** A customer can login using the login page **Manager:** A manager can login using the login page of customer. Post Login homepage will show different links based on role

> Identify the Business Requirement for which TR4 is defined

Step 5: Note the BR (Business Requirement) in Test Case

TestCase #	BR #	TR #	Test Case	Test Steps	Test Data	Expe
1	B1	T94	Verify Login	1) Go to Login Page 2) Enter UserID 3) Enter Password 4) Click Login	id= Guru99 pass= 1234	Login Successful

Step 6: Do above for all Test Cases. Later Extract the First 3 Columns from your Test Suite. RTM in testing is Ready!

Business Requirement #	Technical Requirement #	Test Case ID
B1	T94	1
B2	T95	3
B3	T96	3
B4	T97	4

Requirement Traceability Matrix

Advantage of Requirement Traceability Matrix

- It confirms 100% test coverage

- It highlights any requirements missing or document inconsistencies

- It shows the overall defects or execution status with a focus on business requirements

- It helps in analyzing or estimating the impact on the QA team's work with respect to revisiting or re-working on the test cases

Boundary Value Analysis & Equivalence Partitioning

Practically, due to time and budget considerations, it is not possible to perform exhausting testing for each set of test data, especially when there is a large pool of input combinations.

1. We need an easy way or special techniques that can select test cases intelligently from the pool of test-case, such that all test scenarios are covered.
2. We use two techniques - Equivalence Partitioning & Boundary Value Analysis testing techniques to achieve this.

What is Boundary Testing?

Boundary testing is the process of testing between extreme ends or boundaries between partitions of the input values.

- So these extreme ends like Start- End, Lower- Upper, Maximum-Minimum, Just Inside-Just Outside values are called boundary values and the testing is called "boundary testing".

- The basic idea in boundary value testing is to select input variable values at their:

1. Minimum

2. Just above the minimum

3. A nominal value

4. Just below the maximum

5. Maximum

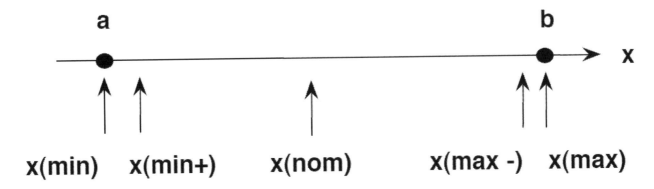

- In Boundary Testing, Equivalence Class Partitioning plays a good role
- Boundary Testing comes after the Equivalence Class Partitioning.

What is Equivalent Class Partitioning?

Equivalent Class Partitioning is a black box technique (code is not visible to tester) which can be applied to all levels of testing like unit, integration, system, etc. In this technique, you divide the set of test condition into a partition that can be considered the same.

- It divides the input data of software into different equivalence data classes.

- You can apply this technique, where there is a range in input field.

Example 1: Equivalence and Boundary Value

- Let's consider the behavior of tickets in the Flight reservation application, while booking a new flight.

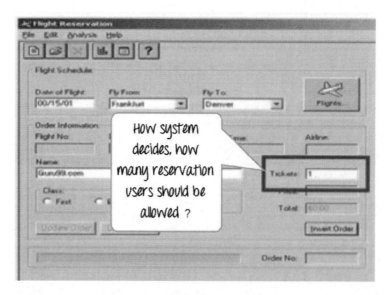

- Ticket values 1 to 10 are considered valid & ticket is booked. While value 11 to 99 are considered invalid for reservation and error message will appear, **"Only ten tickets may be ordered at one time."**

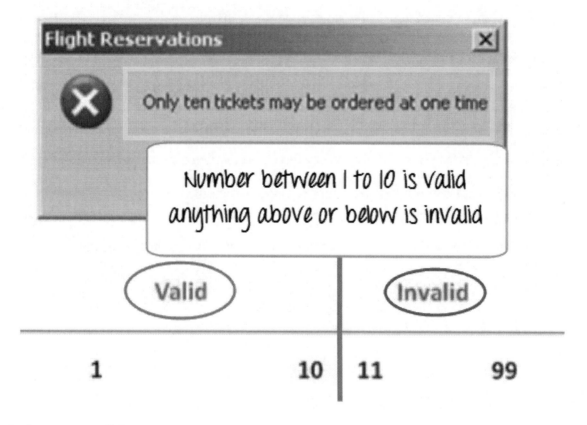

Here is the test condition

1. Any Number greater than 10 entered in the reservation column (let say 11) is considered invalid.

2. Any Number less than 1 that is 0 or below, then it is considered invalid.

3. Numbers 1 to 10 are considered valid

4. Any 3 Digit Number say -100 is invalid.

We cannot test all the possible values because if done, the number of test cases will be more than 100. To address this problem, we use equivalence partitioning hypothesis where we divide the possible values of tickets into groups or sets as shown below where the system behavior can be considered the same.

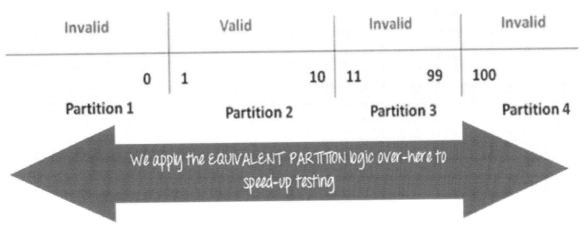

The divided sets are called Equivalence Partitions or Equivalence Classes. Then we pick only one value from each partition for testing. The hypothesis behind this technique is **that if one condition/value in a partition passes all others will also pass**. Likewise, **if one condition in a partition fails, all other conditions in that partition will fail.**

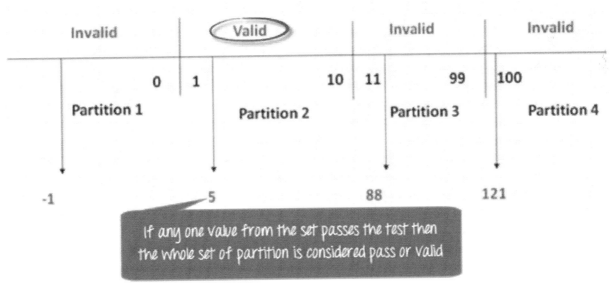

Boundary Value Analysis- in Boundary Value Analysis, you test boundaries between equivalence partitions

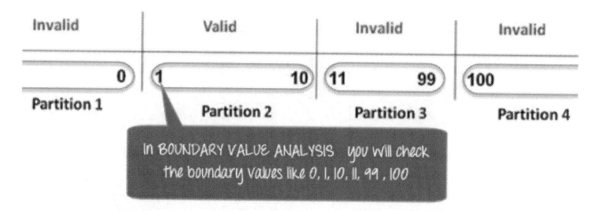

In BOUNDARY VALUE ANALYSIS you will check the boundary values like 0, 1, 10, 11, 99, 100

In our earlier example instead of checking, one value for each partition you will check the values at the partitions like 0, 1, 10, 11 and so on. As you may observe, you test values at **both valid and invalid boundaries**. Boundary Value Analysis is also called **range checking**.

Equivalence partitioning and boundary value analysis are closely related and can be used together at all levels of testing.

Example 2: Equivalence and Boundary Value

Suppose a password field accepts minimum 6 characters and maximum 10 characters

That means results for values in partitions 0-5, 6-10, 11-14 should be equivalent

Test Scenario #	Test Scenario Description	Expected Outcome
1	Enter 0 to 5 characters in password field	System should not accept
2	Enter 6 to 10 characters in password field	System should accept
3	Enter 11 to 14 character in password field	System should not accept

Examples 3: Input Box should accept the Number 1 to 10

Here we will see the Boundary Value Test Cases

Test Scenario Description	Expected Outcome
Boundary Value = 0	System should NOT accept
Boundary Value = 1	System should accept

Boundary Value = 2	System should accept
Boundary Value = 9	System should accept
Boundary Value = 10	System should accept
Boundary Value = 11	System should NOT accept

Why Equivalence & Boundary Analysis Testing

1. This testing is used to reduce very large number of test cases to manageable chunks.

2. Very clear guidelines on determining test cases without compromising on the effectiveness of testing.

3. Appropriate for calculation-intensive applications with large number of variables/inputs

Summary:

- Boundary Analysis testing is used when practically it is impossible to test large pool of test cases individually

- Two techniques - Equivalence Partitioning & Boundary Value Analysis testing techniques is used

- In Equivalence Partitioning, first you divide a set of test condition into a partition that can be considered.

- In Boundary Value Analysis you then test boundaries between equivalence partitions

- Appropriate for calculation-intensive applications with variables that represent physical quantities

Static Testing

What is Static Testing?

Static Testing is a technique by which we can check the defects in software without actually executing it. Its counter-part is Dynamic Testing which checks an application when code is run. Refer this tutorial for a detailed difference between **static and dynamic testing**.

Static testing is done to avoid errors at an early stage of development as it is easier to find sources of failures then failures themselves.

Static testing helps find errors that may not be found by Dynamic Testing.

The two main types of static testing techniques are

- **Manual examinations**: Manual examinations include analysis of code done manually, also known as **REVIEWS.**

- **Automated analysis using tools:** Automated analysis are basically static analysis which is done using tools.

What is Testing Review?

A review in a Static Testing is a process or meeting conducted to find the potential defects in the design of any program. Another significance of review is that all the team members get to know about the progress of the project and sometimes the diversity of thoughts may result in excellent suggestions. Documents are directly examined by people and discrepancies are sorted out.

Reviews can further be classified into four parts:

- Informal reviews

- Walkthroughs

- Technical review

- Inspections

During the Review process four types of participants that take part in testing are:

- **Moderator**: Performs entry check, follow up on rework, coaching team member, schedule the meeting.

- **Author**: Takes responsibility for fixing the defect found and improves the quality of the document

- **Scribe**: It does the logging of the defect during review and attends the review meeting

- **Reviewer**: Check material for defects and inspects

- **Manager**: Decide on the execution of reviews and ensures the review process objectives are met.

Types of defects which can be easier to find during static testing are:

- Deviations from standards

- Non-maintainable code

- Design defects

- Missing requirements

- Inconsistent interface specifications

Usually, the defect discovered during static testing are due to security vulnerabilities, undeclared variables, boundary violations, syntax violations, inconsistent interface, etc.

Why Static Testing

Static testing is performed due to following reasons

- Early defect detection and correction

- Reduced development timescales

- Reduced testing cost and time

- For improvement of development productivity

- To get fewer defect at later stage of testing

What is Tested in Static Testing

In Static Testing, following things are tested

- Unit Test Cases

- Business Requirements Document (BRD)

- Use Cases

- System/Functional Requirements

- Prototype

- Prototype Specification Document

- DB Fields Dictionary Spreadsheet

- Test Data

- Traceability Matrix Document

- User Manual/Training Guides/Documentation

- Test Plan Strategy Document/Test Cases

- Automation/Performance Test Scripts

How Static Testing is Performed

To perform Static Testing, it is done in following ways,

- Carry out the inspection process to completely inspect the design of the application

- Use a checklist for each document under review to ensure all reviews are covered completely

The various activities for performing Static Testing are:

1. **Use Cases Requirements Validation:** It validates that all the end-user actions are identified, as well as any input and output associated with them. The more detailed and thorough the use cases are, the more accurate and comprehensive the test cases can be.

2. **Functional Requirements Validation**: It ensures that the Functional Requirements identify all necessary elements. It also looks at the database functionality, interface listings, and hardware, software, and network requirements.

3. **Architecture Review**: All business level process like server locations, network diagrams, protocol definitions, load balancing, database accessibility, test equipment, etc.

4. **Prototype/Screen Mockup Validation**: This stage includes validation of requirements and use cases.

5. **Field Dictionary Validation**: Every field in the UI is defined well enough to create field level validation test cases. Fields are check for min/max length, list values, error messages, etc.

Static Testing Techniques

- Informal Reviews

- Walkthroughs

- Technical Reviews

- Inspections

- Static Analysis

    o Data Flow

    o Control Flow

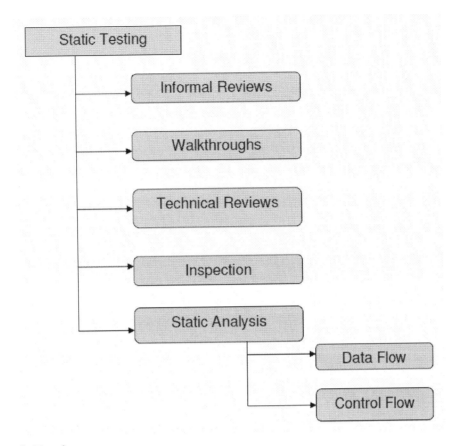

Tools used for Static Testing

Various tools used for Static Testing are as follow,

- Checkstyle

- IntelliJ IDEA

- FindBugs

- Jarchitect

- Soot

- Squale

- ThreadSafe

- SourceMeter

Tips for Successful Static Testing Process

Some useful tips to perform static testing process

- Focus only on things that really count

- Explicitly plan and track review activities. A software walkthrough and inspection are generally composite into peer's reviews

- Train participants

- Resolve people issues

- Keep process formal as the project culture

- Continuous improvement – Process and Tools

- By removing the major delays in test execution, testing cost and time can be reduced

Summary:

- Static testing is to find defects early as possible.

- Static testing not a substitute to dynamic testing, both find different type of defects

- Reviews are effective technique for Static Testing

- Reviews not only help finding defects but also understand missing requirements, design defects, non-maintainable code,

Test Environment

Setting up a right test environment ensures software testing success. Any flaws in this process may lead to extra cost and time to the client.

What is a Test bed?

In general, a test bed is a software development environment. It allows the developers to test their modules without affecting the live production servers. The test bed is not confined to developers only but also used by testers. It is referred as test environment as well.

What is a Test Enviornment?

A testing environment is a setup of software and hardware for the testing teams to execute test cases. In other words, it supports test execution with hardware, software and network configured.

Test bed or test environment is configured as per the need of the Application Under Test. At few occasion, test bed could be the combination of the test environment and the test data it operates.

Key areas to set up in Test Environment

For test environment, key area to set up includes

- System and applications

- Test data

- Database server

- Front end running environment

- Client operating system

- Browser

- Hardware includes Server Operating system

- Network

- Documentation required like reference documents/configuration guides/installation guides/ user manuals

Process of Software Test environment setup

Tests are limited to what can be tested and what not should be tested.

Following people are involved in test environment setup

- System Admins,

- Developers

- Testers

- Sometimes users or techies with an affinity for testing.

The test environment requires setting up of various number of distinct areas like,

Setup of Test Server

Every test may can not be executed on local machine. It may need establishing a test server, which can support applications.

For example: Fedora set up for PHP, **Java** based applications with or without mail servers, cron set up, Java based applications, etc.

Network

Network set up as per the test requirement. It includes,

- Internet setup

- LAN Wifi setup

- Private network setup

It ensures that the congestion that occurs during testing doesn't affect other members. (Developers, designers, content writers, etc.)

Test PC setup

For web testing, you may need to setup different browsers for different testers. For desktop applications, you need various types of OS for different testers PCs.

For example, windows phone app testing may require

- Visual Studio installation

- Windows phone emulator

- Alternatively, assigning a windows phone to the tester.

Bug Reporting

Bug reporting tools should be provided to testers.

Creating Test Data for the Test Environment

Many companies use a separate test environment to test the software product. The common approach used is to copy production data to test. This helps the tester, to detect same issues as live production server, without corrupting the production data.

The approach for copying production data to test data includes,

- Set up production jobs to copy the data to a common test environment

- All PII (Personally Identifiable Information) is modified along with other sensitive data. The PII is replaced with logically correct, but non-personal data.

- Remove data that is irrelevant to your test.

Testers or developers can copy this to their individual test environment. They can modify it as per their requirement.

Privacy is the main issue in copy production data. To overcome privacy issues you should look into obfuscated and anonymized test data.

For Anonymization of data two approaches can be used,

- BlackList: In this approach, all the data fields are left unchanged. Except those fields specified by the users.

- WhiteList: By default, this approach, anonymizes all data fields. Except a list of fields which are allowed to be copied. A whitelisted field implies that it is okay to copy the data as it is and anonymization is not required.

Also, if you are using production data, you need to be smart about how to source data. Querying the database using **SQL** script is an effective approach.

Test Environment Management

Test Environment Management deals with maintainence and upkeep of the test bed.

List of activities by the Test environment management function include,

1. Maintenance of a central repository with all the updated version of test environments.

2. Test environment management as per the test team demands.

3. As per the new requirements creating new environments

4. Monitoring of the environments

5. Updating/deleting outdated test-environments

6. Investigation of issues on the environment

7. Co-ordination till an issue resolution.

Test Environment Checklist

	Hardware	
1	Check whether required equipment for testing is available?	If this is not the case, analyze the supply time!
	Check whether peripheral equipment is available?	Such as scanners, special printers, handhelds, etc.

	Software / connections	
2	Are the needed applications specified?	An application such as excel, word, drawings, etc.
	For the new software does the test environment exist for the organization?	Has the organization experience with use and maintenance of the software?

	Environmental data	
3	Check whether the standard test data sets are available?	With regression test set, consider the defect administration to collect test data.
	Do agreements with the test data owners about the test data exist?	Consider functional maintenance.

Maintenance tools / processes	
4 Check whether a single point of contact exist for test environment maintenance?	If no, prepare a list of all possible members involved in keeping the test environment running. It should include their contact information as well.
Does agreement reached about the readiness and quality of the test environment?	For instance, acceptance criteria, maintenance requirements, etc. Also, check whether other / extra quality attributes for environments are there in agreement.
Do all members involved in the maintenance process are known?	

Beside these, there are few more questions to answer before setting up the test environment.

- Whether to develop an internal Test Environment or to outsource?

- Whether to follow an internal company standard or follow any External (IEE, ISO, etc.)?

- How long test environment be required?

- Differences between the test and production systems and their impact on test validity must be determined.

- Can you re-use any existing setup for other projects in the company?

Challenges in setting up Test Environment Managment

1. **Proper planning on resource usage**

   Ineffective planning for resource usage can affect the actual output. Also, it may lead to conflict between teams.

2. **Remote environment**

   It is possible that Test environment is located geographically apart. In such case the testing team has to rely on the support team for various test assets. (Software, hardware, and other issues).

3. **Elaborate setup time**

   Sometimes test set up gets too elaborated in cases of integration testing.

4. **Shared usage by teams**

If the testing environment is used by development & testing team simultaneously, test results will be corrupted.

5. **Complex test configuration**

   Certain test requires complex test environment configuration. It may pose a challenge to the test team.

Best practices for setting up a Test Environment Management

1. Understand the test requirements thoroughly and educate the test team members.

2. Connectivity should be checked before the initiation of the testing

3. Check for the required hardware and software, licenses

4. Browsers and versions

5. Planning out the Scheduled use of the test environment.

6. Automation tools and their configurations.

Summary:

- A testing environment is a setup of software and hardware on which the test team will conduct the testing

- For test environment, key area to set up includes

  - System and applications

  - Test data

  - Database server

  - Front end running environment, etc.

- Few challenges while setting up test environment include,

  - Remote environment

  - Combined usage between teams

  - Elaborate setup time

  - Ineffective planning for resource usage for integration

  - Complex test configuration

Test Data

What is Test Data? Why is it Important?

Test data is actually the input given to a software program. It represents data that affects or is affected by the execution of the specific module. Some data may be used for positive testing, typically to verify that a given set of input to a given function produces an expected result. Other data may be used for negative testing to test the ability of the program to handle unusual, extreme, exceptional, or unexpected input. Poorly designed testing data may not test all possible test scenarios which will hamper the quality of the software.

What is Test Data Generation? Why test data should be created before test execution?

Depending on your testing environment you may need to CREATE Test Data (Most of the times) or atleast identify a suitable test data for your test cases (is the test data is already created).

Typically test data is created in-sync with the test case it is intended to be used for.

Test Data can be Generated -

- Manually

- Mass copy of data from production to testing environment

- Mass copy of test data from legacy client systems

- Automated Test Data Generation Tools

Typically sample data should be generated before you begin test execution because it is difficult to perform test data management. Since in **many testing environments creating test data takes many**

pre-steps or test environment configurations which is very time consuming. Also If test data generation is done *while* you are in test execution phase you may exceed your testing deadline.

Below are described several testing types together with some suggestions regarding their testing data needs.

Test Data for White Box Testing

In white box testing, test data is derived from direct examination of the code to be tested. Test data may be selected by taking into account the following things:

- It is desirable to cover as many branches as possible; testing data can be generated such that all branches in the program source code are tested at least once

- Path testing: all paths in the program source code are tested at least once - test data can be designed to cover as many cases as possible

- Negative API testing:

    o Testing data may contain invalid parameter types used to call different methods

    o Testing data may consist in invalid combinations of arguments which are used to call the program's methods

Test Data for Performance Testing

Performance testing is the type of testing which is performed in order to determine how fast system responds under a particular workload. The goal of this type of testing is not to find bugs, but to eliminate bottlenecks. An important aspect of performance testing is that the set of sample data used must be very close to *'real' or 'live'* data which is used on production. The following question arises: 'Ok, it's good to test with real data, but how do I obtain this data?' The answer is pretty straightforward: from the people who know the best – **the customers**. They may be able to provide some data they already have or, if they don't have an existing set of data, they may help you by giving feedback regarding how the real-world data might look like. In case you are in a **maintenance testing** project you could copy data from the production environment into the testing bed. It is a good practice to **anonymize** (scramble) sensitive customer data like Social Security Number, Credit Card Numbers, Bank Details etc. while the copy is made.

Test Data for Security Testing

Security testing is the process that determines if an information system protects data from malicious intent. The set of data that need to be designed in order to fully test a software security must cover the following topics:

- **Confidentiality:** All the information provided by clients is held in the strictest confidence and is not shared with any outside parties. As a short example, if an application uses SSL, you can design a set of test data which verifies that the encryption is done correctly.

- **Integrity:** Determine that the information provided by the system is correct. To design suitable test data you can start by taking an in depth look at the design, code, databases and file structures.

- **Authentication:** Represents the process of establishing the identity of a user. Testing data can be designed as different combination of usernames and passwords and its purpose is to check that only the authorized people are able to access the software system.

- **Authorization:** Tells what are the rights of a specific user. Testing data may contain different combination of users, roles and **OPERATIONS** in order to check only users with sufficient privileges are able to perform a particular operation.

Test Data for Black Box Testing

In Black Box Testing the code is not visible to the tester . Your functional test cases can have test data meeting following criteria -

- **No data**: Check system response when no data is submitted

- **Valid data**: Check system response when Valid test data is submitted

- **Invalid data**: Check system response when INVALID test data is submitted

- **Illegal data format**: Check system response when test data is in invalid format

- **Boundary Condition Data set**: Test data meeting bounding value conditions

- **Equivalence Partition Data Set**: Test data qualifying your equivalence partitions.

- **Decision Table Data Set**: Test data qualifying your decision table testing strategy

- **State Transition Test Data Set**: Test data meeting your state transition testing strategy

- **Use Case Test Data**: Test Data in-sync with your use cases.

Note: Depending on the software application to be tested, you may use some or all of the above test data creation

Automated Test Data Generation

In order to generate various sets of data, you can use a gamut of automated test data generation tools. Below are some examples of such tools:

Test Data Generator by **GSApps** can be used for creating intelligent data in almost any database or text file. It enables users to:

- Complete application testing by inflating a database with meaningful data

- Create industry-specific data that can be used for a demonstration

- Protect data privacy by creating a clone of the existing data and masking confidential values

- Accelerate the development cycle by simplifying testing and prototyping

Test Data generator by **DTM**, is a fully customizable utility that generates data, tables (views, procedures etc) for database testing (performance testing, QA testing, load testing or usability testing) purposes.

Datatect is a **SQL** data generator by Banner Software, generates a variety of realistic test data in ASCII flat files or directly generates test data for RDBMS including Oracle, Sybase, **SQL** Server, and Informi.

In conclusion, well-designed testing data allows you to identify and correct serious flaws in functionality. Choice of test data selected must be reevaluated in every phase of a multi-phase product development cycle. So, always keep an eye on it.

What is Defect?

What is Bug?

A bug is the consequence/outcome of a coding fault

What is Defect?

A defect is a variation or deviation from the original business requirements

These two terms have very thin line of differnce, In the Industry both are faults that need to be fixed and so interchangebaly used by some of the **Testing** teams.

When a tester executes the test cases, he might come across the test result which is contradictory to expected result. This variation in the test result is referred as a **Software Defect**. These defects or variation are referred by different names in a different organization like **issues, problem, bug or incidents**.

While reporting the bug to developer, your Bug Report should contain the following information

- **Defect_ID** - Unique identification number for the defect.

- **Defect Description** - Detailed description of the defect including information about the module in which defect was found.

- **Version** - Version of the application in which defect was found.

- **Steps** - Detailed steps along with screenshots with which the developer can reproduce the defects.

- **Date Raised** - Date when the defect is raised

- **Reference**- where in you Provide reference to the documents like . requirements, design, architecture or maybe even screenshots of the error to help understand the defect

- **Detected By** - Name/ID of the tester who raised the defect

- **Status** - Status of the defect , more on this later

- **Fixed by** - Name/ID of the developer who fixed it

- **Date Closed** - Date when the defect is closed

- **Severity** which describes the impact of the defect on the application

- **Priority** which is related to defect fixing urgency. Severity Priority could be High/Medium/Low based on the impact urgency at which the defect should be fixed respectively

Consider the following as a Test Manager

Your team found bugs while testing the Guru99 Banking project.

After a week the developer responds -

In next week the tester responds

As in the above case, if the defect communication is done verbally, soon things become very complicated. To control and effectively manage bugs you need a defect lifecycle.

Defect Management Process

This topic will guide you on how to apply the defect management process to the project Guru99 Bank website. You can follow the below steps to manage defects.

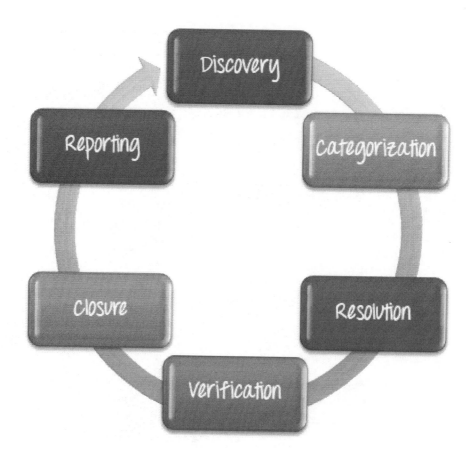

Discovery

In the discovery phase, the project teams have to discover as **many** defects as **possible,** before the end customer can discover it. A defect is said to be discovered and change to status **accepted** when it is acknowledged and accepted by the developers

In the above scenario, the testers discovered 84 defects in the website Guru99.

.

Let's have a look at the following scenario; your testing team discovered some issues in the Guru99 Bank website. They consider them as defects and reported to the development team, but there is a conflict -

In such case, as a Test Manager, what will you do?

In such case, a resolution process should be applied to solve the conflict, you take the role as a judge to decide whether the website problem is a defect or not.

Categorization

Defect categorization help the software developers to prioritize their tasks. That means that this kind of priority helps the developers in fixing those defects first that are highly crucial.

Critical
- The defects that need to be fixed **immediately** because it may cause great damage to the product

High
- The defect impacts the product's **main** features

Medium
- The defect causes **minimal** deviation from product requirement

Low
- The defect has **very minor** affect product operation

Defects are usually categorized by the Test Manager –

Let's do a small exercise as following **Drag & Drop the Defect Priority Below**

Here are the recommended answers

No.	Description	Priority	Explanation
1	The website performance is too slow	High	The performance bug can cause huge inconvenience to user.
2	The login function of the website does not work properly	Critical	Login is one of the main function of the banking website if this feature does not work, it is serious bugs
3	The GUI of the website does not display correctly on mobile devices	Medium	The defect affects the user who use Smartphone to view the website.

| 4 | The website could not remember the user login session | High | This is a serious issue since the user will be able to login but not be able to perform any further transactions |
| 5 | Some links doesn't work | Low | This is an easy fix for development guys and the user can still access the site without these links |

Resolution

Once the defects are accepted and categorized, you can follow the following steps to fix the defect.

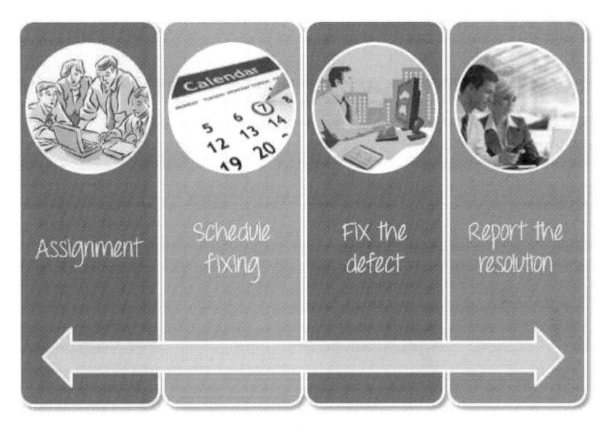

- **Assignment**: Assigned to a developer or other technician to fix, and changed the status to **Responding**.

- **Schedule fixing**: The developer side take charge in this phase. They will create a schedule to fix these defects, depend on the defect priority.

- **Fix the defect**: While the development team is fixing the defects, the Test Manager tracks the process of fixing defect compare to the above schedule.

- **Report the resolution**: Get a report of the resolution from developers when defects are fixed.

Verification

After the development team **fixed** and **reported** the defect, the testing team **verifies** that the defects are actually resolved.

For example, in the above scenario, when the development team reported that they already fixed 61 defects, your team would test again to verify these defects were actually fixed or not.

Closure

Once a defect has been resolved and verified, the defect is changed status as **closed**. If not, you have send a notice to the development to check the defect again.

Reporting

The management board has right to know the defect status. They must understand the defect management process to support you in this project. Therefore, you must report them the current defect situation to get feedback from them.

Important Defect Metrics

Back the above scenario. The developer and test teams have reviews the defects reported. Here is the result of that discussion

How to measure and evaluate the quality of the test execution?

This is a question which every Test Manager wants to know. There are 2 parameters which you can consider as following

| Defect Rejection Ratio | • (No. of defects rejected / Total no. of defects raised) * 100 |
| Defect Leakage Ratio | • (Number defect missed/ total defects of software) * 100 |

In the above scenario, you can calculate the **defection rejection ratio** (DRR) is **20/84 = 0.238 (23.8 %).**

Another example, supposed the Guru99 Bank website has total **64** defects, but your testing team only detect **44** defects i.e. they missed **20** defects. Therefore, you can calculate the defect leakage ratio (DLR) is 20/64 = **0.312** (31.2 %).

Conclusion, the quality of test execution is evaluated via following two parameters

$$Defect\ reject\ ratio\ \ \ = 23.8\%$$
$$Defect\ leakage\ ratio = 31.2\%$$

The smaller value of DRR and DLR is, the better quality of test execution is. What is the ratio range which is **acceptable**? This range could be defined and accepted base in the project target or you may refer the metrics of similar projects.

In this project, the recommended value of acceptable ratio is **5 ~ 10%.** It means the quality of test execution is low. You should find countermeasure to reduce these ratios such as

- **Improve** the testing skills of member.

- **Spend more time** for testing execution, especially for reviewing the test execution results.

Defect Life Cycle
What is Defect Life Cycle?

Defect Life Cycle or Bug Life Cycle is the specific set of states that a Bug goes through from discovery to defect fixation.

The number of states that a defect goes through varies from project to project. Below lifecycle diagram, covers all possible states

- **New:** When a new defect is logged and posted for the first time. It is assigned a status NEW.

- **Assigned:** Once the bug is posted by the tester, the lead of the tester approves the bug and assigns the bug to developer team

- **Open**: The developer starts analyzing and works on the defect fix

- **Fixed**: When developer makes necessary code change and verifies the change, he or she can make bug status as "Fixed."

- **Pending retest**: Once the defect is fixed the developer gives particular code for retesting the code to the tester. Since the testing remains pending from the testers end, the status assigned is "pending request."

- **Retest**: Tester does the retesting of the code at this stage to check whether the defect is fixed by the developer or not and change the status to "Re-test."

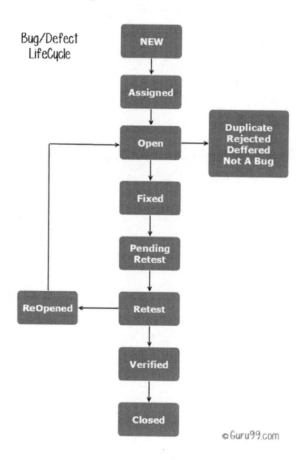

- **Verified**: The tester re-tests the bug after it got fixed by the developer. If there is no bug detected in the software, then the bug is fixed and the status assigned is "verified."

- **Reopen**: If the bug persists even after the developer has fixed the bug, the tester changes the status to "reopened". Once again the bug goes through the life cycle.

- **Closed**: If the bug is no longer exists then tester assigns the status "Closed."

- **Duplicate**: If the defect is repeated twice or the defect corresponds the same concept of the bug, the status is changed to "duplicate."

- **Rejected**: If the developer feels the defect is not a genuine defect then it changes the defect to "rejected."

- **Deferred**: If the present bug is not of a prime priority and if it is expected to get fixed in the next release, then status "Deferred" is assigned to such bugs

- **Not a bug**:If it does not affect the functionality of the application then the status assigned to a bug is "Not a bug".

This training video describes the various stages in a bug aka defect life cycle and its importance with the help of an example

Suppose we have a flight reservation application. Now in order to login into the webpage, you have to enter the correct password "Mercury".

Any wrong password entered for the login page will be addressed as a defect.

While testing the application, tester finds that an error pops out when a wrong password entered into the login page and assigned this error or defect as, **NEW.** This defect is then assigned to development project manager to analyze whether the defect is valid or not. The project manager finds that the defect is not a valid defect.

Defect Life Cycle Explained

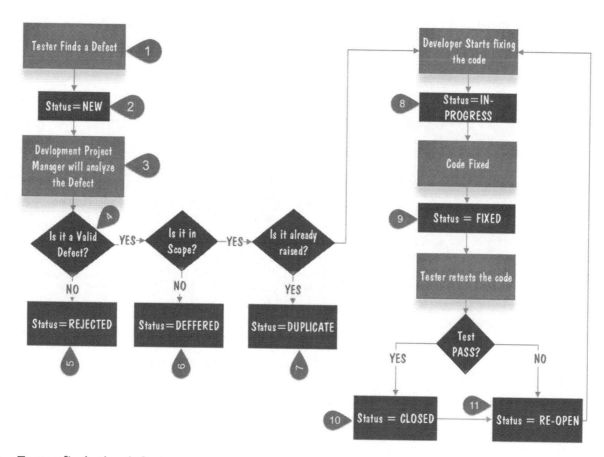

1. Tester finds the defect

2. Status assigned to defect- New

3. Defect is forwarded to Project Manager for analyze

4. Project Manager decides whether defect is valid

5. Here the defect is not valid- status given "Rejected."

6. So, project manager assigns a status **rejected**. If the defect is not rejected then the next step is to check whether it is in scope. Suppose we have another function- email functionality for the same application, and you find a problem with that. But it is not a part of the current release then such defects are assigned as a **postponed or deferred** status.

7. Next, manager verifies whether a similar defect was raised earlier. If yes defect is assigned a status **duplicate**.

8. If no the defect is assigned to the developer who starts fixing the code. During this stage, the defect is assigned a status **in- progress.**

9. Once the code is fixed. Defect is assigned a status **fixed**

10. Next the tester will re-test the code. In case, the test case passes the defect is **closed.** If the test cases fails again, the defect is **re-opened** and assigned to the developer.

11. Consider a situation where during the 1st release of Flight Reservation a defect was found in Fax order that was fixed and assigned a status closed. During the second upgrade release the same defect again re-surfaced. In such cases, a closed defect will be **re-opened.**

That's all to Bug Life Cycle

Section 3: Testing Types

100+ Types of Software Testing

What is a Software Testing Type?

Software Testing Type is a classification of different testing activities into categories, each having, a defined test objective, test strategy, and test deliverables. The goal of having a testing type is to validate the Application Under Test(AUT) for the defined Test Objective.

For instance, the goal of Accessibility testing is to validate the AUT to be accessible by disabled people. So, if your Software solution must be disabled friendly, you check it against Accessibility Test Cases.

A list of **100 types of Software Testing Types** along with definitions. A must read for any QA professional.

1. **Acceptance Testing:** Formal testing conducted to determine whether or not a system satisfies its acceptance criteria and to enable the customer to determine whether or not to accept the system. It is usually performed by the customer.

2. **Accessibility Testing:** Type of testing which determines the usability of a product to the people having disabilities (deaf, blind, mentally disabled etc). The evaluation process is conducted by persons having disabilities.

3. **Active Testing:** Type of testing consisting in introducing test data and analyzing the execution results. It is usually conducted by the testing team.

4. **Agile Testing:** Software testing practice that follows the principles of the agile manifesto, emphasizing testing from the perspective of customers who will utilize the system. It is usually performed by the QA teams.

5. **Age Testing:** Type of testing which evaluates a system's ability to perform in the future. The evaluation process is conducted by testing teams.

6. **Ad-hoc Testing:** Testing performed without planning and documentation - the tester tries to 'break' the system by randomly trying the system's functionality. It is performed by the testing team.

7. **Alpha Testing:** Type of testing a software product or system conducted at the developer's site. Usually it is performed by the end users.

8. **Assertion Testing:** Type of testing consisting in verifying if the conditions confirm the product requirements. It is performed by the testing team.

9. **API Testing:** Testing technique similar to unit testing in that it targets the code level. API Testing differs from unit testing in that it is typically a QA task and not a developer task.

10. **All-pairs Testing:** Combinatorial testing method that tests all possible discrete combinations of input parameters. It is performed by the testing teams.

11. **Automated Testing:** Testing technique that uses automation testing tools to control the environment set-up, test execution and results reporting. It is performed by a computer and is used inside the testing teams.

12. **Basis Path Testing:** A testing mechanism which derives a logical complexity measure of a procedural design and use this as a guide for defining a basic set of execution paths. It is used by testing teams when defining test cases.

13. **Backward Compatibility Testing:** Testing method which verifies the behavior of the developed software with older versions of the test environment. It is performed by testing team.

14. **Beta Testing:** Final testing before releasing application for commercial purpose. It is typically done by end-users or others.

15. **Benchmark Testing:** Testing technique that uses representative sets of programs and data designed to evaluate the performance of computer hardware and software in a given configuration. It is performed by testing teams.

16. **Big Bang Integration Testing:** Testing technique which integrates individual program modules only when everything is ready. It is performed by the testing teams.

17. **Binary Portability Testing:** Technique that tests an executable application for portability across system platforms and environments, usually for conformation to an ABI specification. It is performed by the testing teams.

18. **Boundary Value Testing:** Software testing technique in which tests are designed to include representatives of boundary values. It is performed by the QA testing teams.

19. **Bottom Up Integration Testing:** In bottom-up integration testing, module at the lowest level are developed first and other modules which go towards the 'main' program are integrated and tested one at a time. It is usually performed by the testing teams.

20. **Branch Testing:** Testing technique in which all branches in the program source code are tested at least once. This is done by the developer.

21. **Breadth Testing:** A test suite that exercises the full functionality of a product but does not test features in detail. It is performed by testing teams.

22. **Black box Testing:** A method of software testing that verifies the functionality of an application without having specific knowledge of the application's code/internal structure. Tests are based on requirements and functionality. It is performed by QA teams.

23. **Code-driven Testing:** Testing technique that uses testing frameworks (such as xUnit) that allow the execution of unit tests to determine whether various sections of the code are acting as expected under various circumstances. It is performed by the development teams.

24. **Compatibility Testing:** Testing technique that validates how well a software performs in a particular hardware/software/operating system/network environment. It is performed by the testing teams.

25. **Comparison Testing:** Testing technique which compares the product strengths and weaknesses with previous versions or other similar products. Can be performed by tester, developers, product managers or product owners.

26. **Component Testing:** Testing technique similar to unit testing but with a higher level of integration - testing is done in the context of the application instead of just directly testing a specific method. Can be performed by testing or development teams.

27. **Configuration Testing:** Testing technique which determines minimal and optimal configuration of hardware and software, and the effect of adding or modifying resources such as memory, disk drives and CPU. Usually it is performed by the performance testing engineers.

28. **Condition Coverage Testing:** Type of software testing where each condition is executed by making it true and false, in each of the ways at least once. It is typically made by the automation testing teams.

29. **Compliance Testing:** Type of testing which checks whether the system was developed in accordance with standards, procedures and guidelines. It is usually performed by external companies which offer "Certified OGC Compliant" brand.

30. **Concurrency Testing:** Multi-user testing geared towards determining the effects of accessing the same application code, module or database records. It it usually done by performance engineers.

31. **Conformance Testing:** The process of testing that an implementation conforms to the specification on which it is based. It is usually performed by testing teams.

32. **Context Driven Testing:** An Agile Testing technique that advocates continuous and creative evaluation of testing opportunities in light of the potential information revealed and the value of that information to the organization at a specific moment. It is usually performed by Agile testing teams.

33. **Conversion Testing:** Testing of programs or procedures used to convert data from existing systems for use in replacement systems. It is usually performed by the QA teams.

34. **Decision Coverage Testing:** Type of software testing where each condition/decision is executed by setting it on true/false. It is typically made by the automation testing teams.

35. **Destructive Testing:** Type of testing in which the tests are carried out to the specimen's failure, in order to understand a specimen's structural performance or material behavior under different loads. It is usually performed by QA teams.

36. **Dependency Testing:** Testing type which examines an application's requirements for pre-existing software, initial states and configuration in order to maintain proper functionality. It is usually performed by testing teams.

37. **Dynamic Testing:** Term used in software engineering to describe the testing of the dynamic behavior of code. It is typically performed by testing teams.

38. **Domain Testing:** White box testing technique which contains checkings that the program accepts only valid input. It is usually done by software development teams and occasionally by automation testing teams.

39. **Error-Handling Testing:** Software testing type which determines the ability of the system to properly process erroneous transactions. It is usually performed by the testing teams.

40. **End-to-end Testing:** Similar to system testing, involves testing of a complete application environment in a situation that mimics real-world use, such as interacting with a database, using network communications, or interacting with other hardware, applications, or systems if appropriate. It is performed by QA teams.

41. **Endurance Testing:** Type of testing which checks for memory leaks or other problems that may occur with prolonged execution. It is usually performed by performance engineers.

42. **Exploratory Testing:** Black box testing technique performed without planning and documentation. It is usually performed by manual testers.

43. **Equivalence Partitioning Testing:** Software testing technique that divides the input data of a software unit into partitions of data from which test cases can be derived. it is usually performed by the QA teams.

44. **Fault injection Testing:** Element of a comprehensive test strategy that enables the tester to concentrate on the manner in which the application under test is able to handle exceptions. It is performed by QA teams.

45. **Formal verification Testing:** The act of proving or disproving the correctness of intended algorithms underlying a system with respect to a certain formal specification or property, using formal methods of mathematics. It is usually performed by QA teams.

46. **Functional Testing:** Type of black box testing that bases its test cases on the specifications of the software component under test. It is performed by testing teams.

47. **Fuzz Testing:** Software testing technique that provides invalid, unexpected, or random data to the inputs of a program - a special area of mutation testing. Fuzz testing is performed by testing teams.

48. **Gorilla Testing:** Software testing technique which focuses on heavily testing of one particular module. It is performed by quality assurance teams, usually when running full testing.

49. **Gray Box Testing:** A combination of Black Box and White Box testing methodologies: testing a piece of software against its specification but using some knowledge of its internal workings. It can be performed by either development or testing teams.

50. **Glass box Testing:** Similar to white box testing, based on knowledge of the internal logic of an application's code. It is performed by development teams.

51. **GUI software Testing:** The process of testing a product that uses a graphical user interface, to ensure it meets its written specifications. This is normally done by the testing teams.

52. **Globalization Testing:** Testing method that checks proper functionality of the product with any of the culture/locale settings using every type of international input possible. It is performed by the testing team.

53. **Hybrid Integration Testing:** Testing technique which combines top-down and bottom-up integration techniques in order leverage benefits of these kind of testing. It is usually performed by the testing teams.

54. **Integration Testing:** The phase in software testing in which individual software modules are combined and tested as a group. It is usually conducted by testing teams.

55. **Interface Testing:** Testing conducted to evaluate whether systems or components pass data and control correctly to one another. It is usually performed by both testing and development teams.

56. **Install/uninstall Testing:** Quality assurance work that focuses on what customers will need to do to install and set up the new software successfully. It may involve full, partial or upgrades install/uninstall processes and is typically done by the software testing engineer in conjunction with the configuration manager.

57. **Internationalization Testing:** The process which ensures that product's functionality is not broken and all the messages are properly externalized when used in different languages and locale. It is usually performed by the testing teams.

58. **Inter-Systems Testing:** Testing technique that focuses on testing the application to ensure that interconnection between application functions correctly. It is usually done by the testing teams.

59. **Keyword-driven Testing:** Also known as table-driven testing or action-word testing, is a software testing methodology for automated testing that separates the test creation process into two distinct stages: a Planning Stage and an Implementation Stage. It can be used by either manual or automation testing teams.

60. **Load Testing:** Testing technique that puts demand on a system or device and measures its response. It is usually conducted by the performance engineers.

61. **Localization Testing:** Part of software testing process focused on adapting a globalized application to a particular culture/locale. It is normally done by the testing teams.

62. **Loop Testing:** A white box testing technique that exercises program loops. It is performed by the development teams.

63. **Manual Scripted Testing:** Testing method in which the test cases are designed and reviewed by the team before executing it. It is done by manual testing teams.

64. **Manual-Support Testing:** Testing technique that involves testing of all the functions performed by the people while preparing the data and using these data from automated system. it is conducted by testing teams.

65. **Model-Based Testing:** The application of Model based design for designing and executing the necessary artifacts to perform software testing. It is usually performed by testing teams.

66. **Mutation Testing:** Method of software testing which involves modifying programs' source code or byte code in small ways in order to test sections of the code that are seldom or never accessed during normal tests execution. It is normally conducted by testers.

67. **Modularity-driven Testing:** Software testing technique which requires the creation of small, independent scripts that represent modules, sections, and functions of the application under test. It is usually performed by the testing team.

68. **Non-functional Testing:** Testing technique which focuses on testing of a software application for its non-functional requirements. Can be conducted by the performance engineers or by manual testing teams.

69. **Negative Testing:** Also known as "test to fail" - testing method where the tests' aim is showing that a component or system does not work. It is performed by manual or automation testers.

70. **Operational Testing:** Testing technique conducted to evaluate a system or component in its operational environment. Usually it is performed by testing teams.

71. **Orthogonal array Testing:** Systematic, statistical way of testing which can be applied in user interface testing, system testing, regression testing, configuration testing and performance testing. It is performed by the testing team.

72. **Pair Testing:** Software development technique in which two team members work together at one keyboard to test the software application. One does the testing and the other analyzes or reviews the testing. This can be done between one Tester and Developer or **Business Analyst** or between two testers with both participants taking turns at driving the keyboard.

73. **Passive Testing:** Testing technique consisting in monitoring the results of a running system without introducing any special test data. It is performed by the testing team.

74. **Parallel Testing:** Testing technique which has the purpose to ensure that a new application which has replaced its older version has been installed and is running correctly. It is conducted by the testing team.

75. **Path Testing:** Typical white box testing which has the goal to satisfy coverage criteria for each logical path through the program. It is usually performed by the development team.

76. **Penetration Testing:** Testing method which evaluates the security of a computer system or network by simulating an attack from a malicious source. Usually they are conducted by specialized penetration testing companies.

77. **Performance Testing:** Functional testing conducted to evaluate the compliance of a system or component with specified performance requirements. It is usually conducted by the performance engineer.

78. **Qualification Testing:** Testing against the specifications of the previous release, usually conducted by the developer for the consumer, to demonstrate that the software meets its specified requirements.

79. **Ramp Testing:** Type of testing consisting in raising an input signal continuously until the system breaks down. It may be conducted by the testing team or the performance engineer.

80. **Regression Testing:** Type of software testing that seeks to uncover software errors after changes to the program (e.g. bug fixes or new functionality) have been made, by retesting the program. It is performed by the testing teams.

81. **Recovery Testing:** Testing technique which evaluates how well a system recovers from crashes, hardware failures, or other catastrophic problems. It is performed by the testing teams.

82. **Requirements Testing:** Testing technique which validates that the requirements are correct, complete, unambiguous, and logically consistent and allows designing a necessary and sufficient set of test cases from those requirements. It is performed by QA teams.

83. **Security Testing:** A process to determine that an information system protects data and maintains functionality as intended. It can be performed by testing teams or by specialized security-testing companies.

84. **Sanity Testing:** Testing technique which determines if a new software version is performing well enough to accept it for a major testing effort. It is performed by the testing teams.

85. **Scenario Testing:** Testing activity that uses scenarios based on a hypothetical story to help a person think through a complex problem or system for a testing environment. It is performed by the testing teams.

86. **Scalability Testing:** Part of the battery of non-functional tests which tests a software application for measuring its capability to scale up - be it the user load supported, the number of transactions, the data volume etc. It is conducted by the performance engineer.

87. **Statement Testing:** White box testing which satisfies the criterion that each statement in a program is executed at least once during program testing. It is usually performed by the development team.

88. **Static Testing:** A form of software testing where the software isn't actually used it checks mainly for the sanity of the code, algorithm, or document. It is used by the developer who wrote the code.

89. **Stability Testing:** Testing technique which attempts to determine if an application will crash. It is usually conducted by the performance engineer.

90. **Smoke Testing:** Testing technique which examines all the basic components of a software system to ensure that they work properly. Typically, smoke testing is conducted by the testing team, immediately after a software build is made .

91. **Storage Testing:** Testing type that verifies the program under test stores data files in the correct directories and that it reserves sufficient space to prevent unexpected termination resulting from lack of space. It is usually performed by the testing team.

92. **Stress Testing:** Testing technique which evaluates a system or component at or beyond the limits of its specified requirements. It is usually conducted by the performance engineer.

93. **Structural Testing:** White box testing technique which takes into account the internal structure of a system or component and ensures that each program statement performs its intended function. It is usually performed by the software developers.

94. **System Testing:** The process of testing an integrated hardware and software system to verify that the system meets its specified requirements. It is conducted by the testing teams in both development and target environment.

95. **System integration Testing:** Testing process that exercises a software system's coexistence with others. It is usually performed by the testing teams.

96. **Top Down Integration Testing:** Testing technique that involves starting at the stop of a system hierarchy at the user interface and using stubs to test from the top down until the entire system has been implemented. It is conducted by the testing teams.

97. **Thread Testing:** A variation of top-down testing technique where the progressive integration of components follows the implementation of subsets of the requirements. It is usually performed by the testing teams.

98. **Upgrade Testing:** Testing technique that verifies if assets created with older versions can be used properly and that user's learning is not challenged. It is performed by the testing teams.

99. **Unit Testing:** Software verification and validation method in which a programmer tests if individual units of source code are fit for use. It is usually conducted by the development team.

100. **User Interface Testing:** Type of testing which is performed to check how user-friendly the application is. It is performed by testing teams.

Bonus !!! Its always good to know a few extra

101. **Usability Testing:** Testing technique which verifies the ease with which a user can learn to operate, prepare inputs for, and interpret outputs of a system or component. It is usually performed by end users.

102. **Volume Testing:** Testing which confirms that any values that may become large over time (such as accumulated counts, logs, and data files), can be accommodated by the program and will not cause the program to stop working or degrade its operation in any manner. It is usually conducted by the performance engineer.

103. **Vulnerability Testing:** Type of testing which regards application security and has the purpose to prevent problems which may affect the application integrity and stability. It can be performed by the internal testing teams or outsourced to specialized companies.

104. **White box Testing:** Testing technique based on knowledge of the internal logic of an application's code and includes tests like coverage of code statements, branches, paths, conditions. It is performed by software developers.

105. **Workflow Testing:** Scripted end-to-end testing technique which duplicates specific workflows which are expected to be utilized by the end-user. It is usually conducted by testing teams.

Unit Testing

What is Unit Testing?

Unit testing of software applications is done during the development (coding) of an application.

The objective of unit testing is to isolate a section of code and verify its correctness. In procedural programming a unit may be an individual function or procedure

The goal of unit testing is to isolate each part of the program and show that the individual parts are correct. Unit testing is usually performed by the developer.

Why do Unit Testing? Why it is important?

Sometimes software developers attempt to save time by doing minimal unit testing. This is a myth because skimping on unit testing leads to higher defect fixing costs during system testing, integration testing and even beta testing after the application is completed. Proper unit testing done during the development stage saves both time and money in the end.

How to Create Unit Test Cases

Unit testing is commonly automated, but may still be performed manually. The IEEE does not favor one over the other. A manual approach to unit testing may employ a step-by-step instructional document.

Under the automated approach-

- A developer could write another section of code in the application just to test the function. They would later comment out and finally remove the test code when the application is done.

- They could also isolate the function to test it more rigorously. This is a more thorough unit testing practice that involves copy and pasting the function to its own testing environment to other than its natural environment. Isolating the code helps in revealing unnecessary dependencies between the code being tested and other units or data spaces in the product. These dependencies can then be eliminated.

A coder may use a UnitTest Framework to develop automated test cases. Using an automation framework, the developer codes criteria into the test to verify the correctness of the unit. During execution of the test cases, the framework logs those that fail any criterion. Many frameworks will also automatically flag and report in a summary these failed test cases. Depending upon the severity of a failure, the framework may halt subsequent testing.

Mock Objects

Unit testing relies on mock objects being created to test sections of code that are not yet part of a complete application. Mock objects fill in for the missing parts of the program. For example, you might have a function that needs variables or objects that are not created yet. In unit testing, those will be accounted for in the form of mock objects created solely for the purpose of the unit testing done on that section of code.

Unit Testing Tools

There are several automated tools available to assist with unit testing. We will provide a few examples below:

- Rational Software - Rational Software by IBM has a unittest feature known as "Rational Test Realtime". The software contains a complete range of testing tools for much more than just unit testing. It is used for Ada, Java, C and C++. It creates unit tests by reverse engineering the software. Operating systems it supports include Windows, Linux, Solaris, HP-UX and AIX. Go to **http://www-01.ibm.com/software/rational/** to learn more.

- JavaScript Assertion Unit- Also known as jsAsserUnit, this Freeware **JavaScript** unit testing tool can be used on any platform that supports JavaScript. It is available at **http://jsassertunit.sourceforge.net/docs/index.html**

- CUT - CUT is a Freeware unittest tool for C, C++ and Objective C. It is great for embedded software testing frameworks and desktop applications on **Linux** and Windows operating systems. Learn more at sourceforge.net by going to **http://sourceforge.net/projects/cut/**.

- Dotunit - Dotunit is a .net framework Freeware unit testing tool. Part of **Junit** on the Microsoft .net framework, Dotunit is used for automating unit testing on windows systems. This is another tool from sourceforge.net, so look for it at: **http://dotunit.sourceforge.net/**

Those are just a few of the available unit testing tools. There are lots more, especially for C languages and Java, but you are sure to find a unit testing tool for your programming needs regardless of the language you use.

Extreme Programming & Unit Testing

Unit testing in Extreme Programming involves the extensive use of testing frameworks. A unit test framework is used in order to create automated unit tests. Unit testing frameworks are not unique to extreme programming, but they are essential to it. Below we look at some of what extreme programming brings to the world of unit testing:

- Tests are written before the code

- Rely heavily on testing frameworks

- All classes in the applications are tested

- Quick and easy integration is made possible

Unit Testing Myth

Myth: It requires time and I am always overscheduled

My code is rock solid! I do not need unit tests.

Myths by their very nature are false assumptions. These assumptions lead to a vicious cycle as follows -

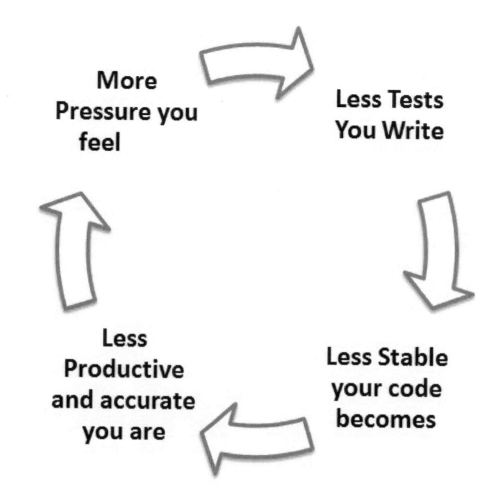

Truth is Unit testing increase the speed of development.

Programmers think that integration testing will catch all errors and do not unit test. Once units are integrated, very simple errors which could have very easily found and fixed in unit tested take very long time to be traced and fixed.

Unit Testing Benefits and Advantage

- Developers looking to learn what functionality is provided by a unit and how to use it can look at the unit tests to gain a basic understanding of the unit API.

- Unit testing allows the programmer to refactor code at a later date, and make sure the module still works correctly (i.e. Regression testing). The procedure is to write test cases for all functions and methods so that whenever a change causes a fault, it can be quickly identified and fixed.

- Due to the modular nature of the unit testing, we can tests parts of project without waiting for others to be completed.

Unit Testing Limitations

- Unit testing can't be expected to catch every error in a program. It is not possible to evaluate all execution paths even in the most trivial programs

- Unit testing by its very nature focuses on a unit of code. Hence it can't catch integration errors or broad system level errors.

It's recommended unit testing be used in conjunction with other testing activities.

Unit Testing Techniques

- Structural Techniques

- Functional Testing Techniques

- Error Based Techniques

Unit Testing Best Practices

- Unit Test cases should be independent. In case of any enhancements or change in requirements, unit test cases should not be affected.

- Test only one code at a time.

- Follow clear and consistent naming conventions for your unit tests

- In case of change in code in any module, ensure there is a corresponding unit test case for the module and the module passes the tests before changing the implementation

- Bugs identified during unit testing must be fixed before proceeding to the next phase in SDLC

- Adopt a "test as your code" approach. The more code you write without testing the more paths you have to check for errors.

Keep on a straight path with proper unit testing.

The more code you write without testing, the more paths you have to check for errors.

Summary

As you can see, there can be a lot involved in unit testing. It can be complex or rather simple depending on the application being tested and the testing strategies, tools and philosophies used. Unit testing is always necessary on some level. That is a certainty.

INTEGRATION Testing

What is Integration Testing?

In Integration Testing, individual software modules are integrated logically and tested as a group.

A typical software project consists of multiple software modules, coded by different programmers.

Integration testing focuses on checking data communication amongst these modules.

Hence it is also termed as **'I & T'** (Integration and Testing), **'String Testing'** and sometimes 'Thread Testing'.

Why do Integration Testing?:

Although each software module is unit tested, defects still exist for various reasons like

- A Module in general is designed by an individual software developer whose understanding and programming logic may differ from other programmers. Integration testing becomes necessary to verify the software modules work in unity

- At the time of module development, there are wide chances of change in requirements by the clients. These new requirements may not be unit tested and hence system integration testing becomes necessary.

- Interfaces of the software modules with the database could be erroneous

- External Hardware interfaces, if any, could be erroneous

- Inadequate exception handling could cause issues.

Integration Test Case:

Integration Test case differs from other test cases in the sense it **focuses mainly on the interfaces & flow of data/information between the modules**. Here priority is to be given for the **integrating links** rather than the unit functions which are already tested.

Sample Integration Test Cases for the following scenario:Application has 3 modules say 'Login Page', 'Mail box' and 'Delete mails' and each of them are integrated logically.

Here do not concentrate much on the Login Page testing as it's already been done in Unit Testing. But check how it's linked to the Mail Box Page.

Similarly Mail Box: Check its integration to the Delete Mails Module.

Test Case ID	Test Case Objective	Test Case Description	Expected Result

1	Check the interface link between the Login and Mailbox module	Enter login credentials and click on the Login button	To be directed to the Mail Box
2	Check the interface link between the Mailbox and Delete Mails Module	From Mail box select the an email and click delete button	Selected email should appear in the Deleted/Trash folder

Approaches/Methodologies/Strategies of Integration Testing:

The Software Industry uses variety of strategies to execute Integration testing , viz.

- Big Bang Approach :

- Incremental Approach: which is further divided into following

  - Top Down Approach

  - Bottom Up Approach

  - Sandwich Approach - Combination of Top Down and Bottom Up

Below are the different strategies, the way they are executed and their limitations as well advantages.

Big Bang Approach:

Here all component are integrated together at **once**, and then tested.

Advantages:

- Convenient for small systems.

Disadvantages:

- Fault Localization is difficult.

- Given the sheer number of interfaces that need to be tested in this approach, some interfaces links to be tested could be missed easily.

- Since the integration testing can commence only after "all" the modules are designed, testing team will have less time for execution in the testing phase.

- Since all modules are tested at once, high risk critical modules are not isolated and tested on priority. Peripheral modules which deal with user interfaces are also not isolated and tested on priority.

Incremental Approach:

In this approach, testing is done by joining two or more modules that are **LOGICALLY RELATED**. Then the other related modules are added and tested for the proper functioning. Process continues until all of the modules are joined and tested successfully.

This process is carried out by using dummy programs called **Stubs and Drivers**. Stubs and Drivers do not implement the entire programming logic of the software module but just simulate data communication with the calling module.

Stub: Is called by the Module under Test.

Driver: Calls the Module to be tested.

Incremental Approach in turn is carried out by two different Methods:

- **Bottom Up**

- **Top Down**

Bottom up Integration

In the bottom up strategy, each module at lower levels is tested with higher modules until all modules are tested. It takes help of Drivers for testing

Diagrammatic Representation:

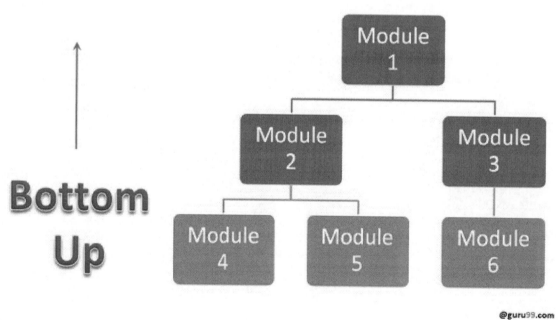

Advantages:

- Fault localization is easier.

- No time is wasted waiting for all modules to be developed unlike Big-bang approach

Disadvantages:

- Critical modules (at the top level of software architecture) which control the flow of application are tested last and may be prone to defects.

- Early prototype is not possible

Top down Integration:

In Top to down approach, testing takes place from top to down following the control flow of the software system.

Takes help of stubs for testing.

Diagrammatic Representation:

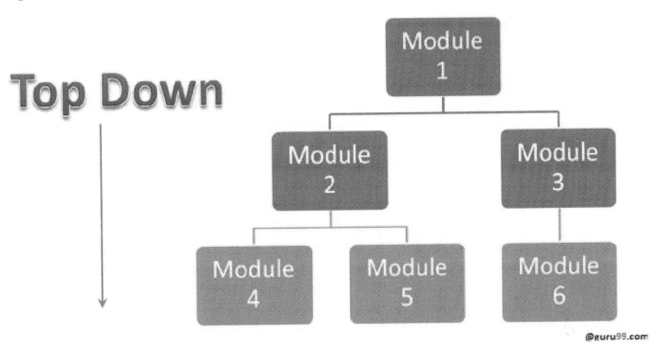

Advantages:

- Fault Localization is easier.

- Possibility to obtain an early prototype.

- Critical Modules are tested on priority; major design flaws could be found and fixed first.

Disadvantages:

- Needs many Stubs.

- Modules at lower level are tested inadequately.

Integration Testing Procedure

The integration test procedure irrespective of the test strategies (discussed above):

1. Prepare the Integration Tests Plan

2. Design the Test Scenarios, Cases, and Scripts.

3. Executing the test Cases followed by reporting the defects.

4. Tracking & re-testing the defects.

5. Steps 3 and 4 are repeated until the completion of Integration is successfully.

Brief Description of Integration Test Plans:

It includes following attributes:

- Methods/Approaches to test (as discussed above).

- Scopes and Out of Scopes Items of Integration Testing.

- Roles and Responsibilities.

- Pre-requisites for Integration testing.

- Testing environment.

- Risk and Mitigation Plans.

Entry and Exit Criteria.

Entry and Exit Criteria to Integration testing phase in any software development model

Entry Criteria:

- Unit Tested Components/Modules

- All High prioritized bugs fixed and closed

- All Modules to be code completed and integrated successfully.

- Integration tests Plan, test case, scenarios to be signed off and documented.

- Required Test Environment to be set up for Integration testing

Exit Criteria:

- Successful Testing of Integrated Application.

- Executed Test Cases are documented

- All High prioritized bugs fixed and closed

- Technical documents to be submitted followed by release Notes.

Best Practices/ Guidelines for Integration Testing

- First determine the Integration Test Strategy that could be adopted and later prepare the test cases and test data accordingly.

- Study the Architecture design of the Application and identify the Critical Modules. These need to be tested on priority.

- Obtain the interface designs from the Architectural team and create test cases to verify all of the interfaces in detail. Interface to database/external hardware/software application must be tested in detail.

- After the test cases, it's the test data which plays the critical role.

- Always have the mock data prepared, prior to executing. Do not select test data while executing the test cases.

System Testing

What is System Testing?

System testing is the testing of a complete and fully integrated software product.

Usually software is only one element of a larger computer based system. Ultimately, software is interfaced with other software/hardware systems.

System testing is actually a series of different tests whose sole purpose is to exercise the full computer based system.

Two Category of Software Testing

- Black Box Testing

- White Box Testing

System test falls under the **black box testing** category of software testing.

White box testing is the testing of the internal workings or code of a software application. In contrast, black box or system testing is the opposite. System test involves the external workings of the software from the user's perspective.

What do you verify in System Testing ?

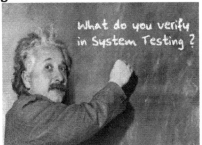

System testing involves testing the software code for following

- **Testing the fully integrated applications** including external peripherals in order to check how components interact with one another and with the system as a whole. This is also called End to End testing scenario..

- Verify thorough testing of every input in the application to check for desired outputs.

- Testing of the user's experience with the application. .

That is a very basic description of what is involved in system testing. You need to build detailed test cases and test suites that test each aspect of the application as seen from the outside without looking at the actual source code.

Software Testing Hierarchy

As with almost any technical process, software testing has a prescribed order in which things should be done. The following is a list of software testing categories arranged in chronological order. These are the steps taken to fully test new software in preparation for marketing it:

- **Unit testing** - testing performed on each module or block of code during development. Unit testing is normally done by the programmer who writes the code.

- **Integration testing** - testing done before, during and after integration of a new module into the main software package. This involves testing of each individual code module. One piece of software can contain several modules which are often created by several different programmers. It is crucial to test each module's effect on the entire program model.

- **System testing** - testing done by a professional testing agent on the completed software product before it is introduced to the market.

- **Acceptance testing** - beta testing of the product done by the actual end users.

Different Types of System Testing

There are more than 50 types of System Testing. For an exhaustive list of software testing types click **here**. Below we have listed types of system testing a large software development company would typically use

1. **Usability Testing** - Usability testing mainly focuses on the user's ease to use the application, flexibility in handling controls and ability of the system to meet its objectives

2. **Load Testing** - Load testing is necessary to know that a software solution will perform under real-life loads.

3. **Regression Testing-** - Regression testing involves testing done to make sure none of the changes made over the course of the development process have caused new bugs. It also makes sure no old bugs appear from the addition of new software modules over time.

4. **Recovery Testing -** Recovery testing is done to demonstrate a software solution is reliable, trustworthy and can successfully recoup from possible crashes.

5. **Migration Testing -** Migration testing is done to ensure that the software can be moved from older system infrastructures to current system infrastructures without any issues.

6. **Functional Testing -** Also known as functional completeness testing, functional testing involves trying to think of any possible missing functions. Testers might make a list of additional functionalities that a product could have to improve it during functional testing.

7. **Hardware/Software Testing -** IBM refers to Hardware/Software testing as "HW/SW Testing". This is when the tester focuses his/her attention on the interactions between the hardware and software during system testing.

What Types of System Testing Should Testers Use?

There are over 50 different types of system testing. The specific types used by a tester depend on several variables. Those variables include:

- **Who the tester works for** - This is a major factor in determining the types of system testing a tester will use. Methods used by large companies are different than that used by medium and small companies.

- **Time available for testing** - Ultimately, all 50 testing types could be used. Time is often what limits us to using only the types that are most relevant for the software project.

- **Resources available to the tester** - Of course some testers will not have necessary resources to conduct a testing type. For example if you are a tester working for a large software development firm, you are likely to have expensive automated testing software not available to others.

- **Software Tester's Education** - There is a certain learning curve for each type of software testing available. To use some of the software involved, a tester has to learn how to use it.

- **Testing Budget** - Money becomes a factor not just for smaller companies and individual software developers but large companies as well.

Regression Testing

What is Regression Testing?

Regression testing is defined as a type of software testing to confirm that a recent program or code change has not adversely affected existing features.

Regression testing is nothing but full or partial selection of already executed test cases which are re-executed to ensure existing functionalities work fine.

This testing is done to make sure that new code changes should not have side effects on the existing functionalities. It ensures that old code still works once the new code changes are done.

Need of Regression Testing

Regression Testing is required when there is a

- Change in requirements and code is modified according to the requirement
- New feature is added to the software
- Defect fixing
- Performance issue fix

Regression Testing Techniques

Software maintenance is an activity which includes enhancements, error corrections, optimization and deletion of existing features. These modifications may cause the system to work incorrectly. Therefore, Regression Testing becomes necessary. Regression Testing can be carried out using following techniques:

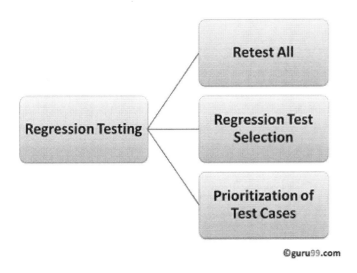

©guru99.com

Retest All

- This is one of the methods for regression testing in which all the tests in the existing test bucket or suite should be re-executed. This is very expensive as it requires huge time and resources.

Regression Test Selection

- Instead of re-executing the entire test suite, it is better to select part of test suite to be run

- Test cases selected can be categorized as 1) Reusable Test Cases 2) Obsolete Test Cases.

- Re-usable Test cases can be used in succeeding regression cycles.

- Obsolete Test Cases can't be used in succeeding cycles.

Prioritization of Test Cases

- Prioritize the test cases depending on business impact, critical & frequently used functionalities. Selection of test cases based on priority will greatly reduce the regression test suite.

Selecting test cases for regression testing

It was found from industry data that good number of the defects reported by customers were due to last minute bug fixes creating side effects and hence selecting the test case for regression testing is an art and not that easy. Effective Regression Tests can be done by selecting following test cases -

- Test cases which have frequent defects

- Functionalities which are more visible to the users

- Test cases which verify core features of the product

- Test cases of Functionalities which has undergone more and recent changes

- All Integration Test Cases

- All Complex Test Cases

- Boundary value test cases

- Sample of Successful test cases

- Sample of Failure test cases

Regression Testing Tools

If your software undergoes frequent changes, regression testing costs will escalate.

In such cases, Manual execution of test cases increases test execution time as well as costs.

Automation of regression test cases is the smart choice in such cases.

Extent of automation depends on the number of test cases that remain re-usable for successive regression cycles.

Following are most important tools used for both functional and regression testing:

Selenium: This is an open source tool used for automating web applications. **Selenium** can be used for browser based regression testing.

Quick Test Professional (QTP): HP Quick Test Professional is automated software designed to automate functional and regression test cases. It uses **VBScript** language for automation. It is a Data driven, Keyword based tool.

Rational Functional Tester (RFT): IBM's rational functional tester is a **Java** tool used to automate the test cases of software applications. This is primarily used for automating regression test cases and it also integrates with Rational Test Manager.

Regression Testing and Configuration Management

Configuration Management during Regression Testing becomes imperative in Agile Environments where code is being continuously modified. To ensure effective regression tests, observe the following :

- Code being regression tested should be under a configuration management tool

- No changes must be allowed to code, during the regression test phase. Regression test code must be kept immune to developer changes.

- The database used for regression testing must be isolated. No database changes must be allowed

Difference between Re-Testing and Regression Testing:

Retesting means testing the functionality or bug again to ensure the code is fixed. If it is not fixed, defect needs to be re-opened. If fixed, defect is closed.

Regression testing means testing your software application when it undergoes a code change to ensure that the new code has not affected other parts of the software.

Also, Check out the complete list of differences over **here** .

Challenges in Regression Testing:

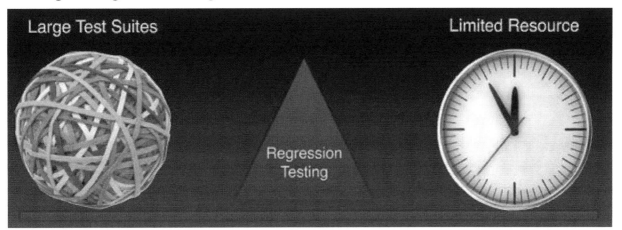

Following are the major testing problems for doing regression testing:

- With successive regression runs, test suites become fairly large. Due to time and budget constraints, the entire regression test suite cannot be executed

- Minimizing test suite while achieving maximum test coverage remains a challenge

- Determination of frequency of Regression Tests, i.e., after every modification or every build update or after a bunch of bug fixes, is a challenge.

Practical Application of Regression Testing with a Video

Conclusion:

An effective regression strategy, save organizations both time and money. As per one of the case study in banking domain, regression saves up to 60% time in bug fixes(which would have been caught by regression tests) and 40% in money

Sanity Testing & Smoke Testing

Smoke and Sanity testing are the most misunderstood topics in Software Testing. There is enormous amount of literature on the subject, but most of them are confusing. The following article makes an attempt to address the confusion.

The key differences between Smoke and Sanity Testing can be learned with the help of following diagram -

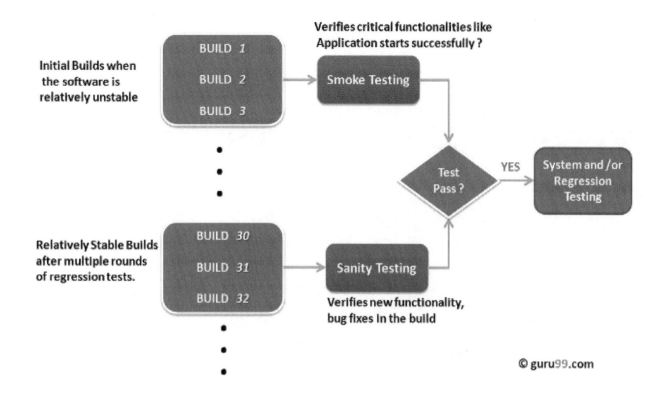

To appreciate the above diagram, lets first understand -

What is a Software Build?

If you are developing a simple computer program which consists of only one source code file, you merely need to compile and link this one file, to produce an executable file. This process is very simple.

Usually this is not the case. A typical Software Project consists of hundreds or even thousands of source code files. Creating an executable program from these source files is a complicated and time-consuming task.

You need to use "build" software to create an executable program and the process is called " SOFTWARE BUILD"

What is Smoke Testing?

Smoke Testing is a kind of Software Testing performed after software build to ascertain that the critical functionalities of the program is working fine. It is executed "before" any detailed functional or regression tests are executed on the software build. The purpose is to reject a badly broken application, so that the QA team does not waste time installing and testing the software application.

In Smoke Testing, the test cases chosen cover the most important functionality or component of the system. The objective is not to perform exhaustive testing, but to verify that the critical functionalities of the system is working fine.

For Example a typical smoke test would be - Verify that the application launches successfully, Check that the GUI is responsive ... etc.

What is Sanity Testing?

Sanity testing is a kind of Software Testing performed after receiving a software build, with minor changes in code, or functionality, to ascertain that the bugs have been fixed and no further issues are introduced due to these changes. The goal is to determine that the proposed functionality works roughly as expected. If sanity test fails, the build is rejected to save the time and costs involved in a more rigorous testing.

The objective is "not" to verify thoroughly the new functionality, but to determine that the developer has applied some rationality (sanity) while producing the software. For instance, if your scientific calculator gives the result of 2 + 2 =5! Then, there is no point testing the advanced functionalities like sin 30 + cos 50.

Smoke Testing Vs Sanity Testing - Key Differences

Smoke Testing	Sanity Testing
Smoke Testing is performed to ascertain that the critical functionalities of the program is working fine	Sanity Testing is done to check the new functionality / bugs have been fixed
The objective of this testing is to verify the "stability" of the system in order to proceed with more rigorous testing	The objective of the testing is to verify the "rationality" of the system in order to proceed with more rigorous testing
This testing is performed by the developers or testers	Sanity testing is usually performed by testers
Smoke testing is usually documented or scripted	Sanity testing is usually not documented and is unscripted
Smoke testing is a subset of Regression testing	Sanity testing is a subset of Acceptance testing
Smoke testing exercises the entire system from end to end	Sanity testing exercises only the particular component of the entire system
Smoke testing is like General Health Check Up	Sanity Testing is like specialized health check up

Points to note.

- Both sanity tests and smoke tests are ways to avoid wasting time and effort by quickly determining whether an application is too flawed to merit any rigorous testing.

- Sanity Testing is also called tester acceptance testing.

- Smoke testing performed on a particular build is also known as a build verification test.

- One of the best industry practice is to conduct a Daily build and smoke test in software projects.

- Both smoke and sanity tests can be executed manually or using an automation tool. When automated tools are used, the tests are often initiated by the same process that generates the build itself.

- As per the needs of testing, you may have to execute both Sanity and Smoke Tests on the software build. In such cases, you will first execute Smoke tests and then go ahead with Sanity Testing. In industry, test cases for Sanity Testing are commonly combined with that for smoke tests, to speed up test execution. Hence, it's a common that the terms are often confused and used interchangeably

Performance Testing

What is Performance Testing?

Performance testing is a type of testing to ensure software applications will perform well under their expected workload.

Features and Functionality supported by a software system is not the only concern. A software application's performance like its response time, reliability, resource usage and scalability do matter. The goal of performance testing is not to find bugs but to eliminate performance bottlenecks.

The focus of Performance testing is checking a software program's

- Speed - Determines whether the application responds quickly

- Scalability - Determines maximum user load the software application can handle.

- Stability - Determines if the application is stable under varying loads

Performance testing is popularly called as "Perf Testing" and is a subset of performance engineering.

Why do Performance Testing?

Performance testing is done to provide stakeholders with information about their application regarding speed, stability and scalability. More importantly, performance testing uncovers what needs to be improved before the product goes to market. Without performance testing, software is likely to suffer from issues such as: running slow while several users use it simultaneously, inconsistencies across different operating systems and poor usability. Performance testing will determine whether or not their software meets speed, scalability and stability requirements under expected workloads. Applications sent to market with poor performance metrics due to non existent or poor performance testing are likely to gain a bad reputation and fail to meet expected sales goals. Also, mission critical applications like space launch programs or life saving medical equipments should be performance tested to ensure that they run for a long period of time without deviations.

Types of Performance Testing

- **Load testing** - checks the application's ability to perform under anticipated user loads. The objective is to identify performance bottlenecks before the software application goes live.

- **Stress testing** - involves testing an application under extreme workloads to see how it handles high traffic or data processing. The objective is to identify breaking point of an application.

- **Endurance testing** - is done to make sure the software can handle the expected load over a long period of time.

- **Spike testing** - tests the software's reaction to sudden large spikes in the load generated by users.

- **Volume testing** - Under Volume Testing large no. of. Data is populated in database and the overall software system's behavior is monitored. The objective is to check software application's performance under varying database volumes.

- **Scalability testing** - The objective of scalability testing is to determine the software application's effectiveness in "scaling up" to support an increase in user load. It helps plan capacity addition to your software system.

Common Performance Problems

Most performance problems revolve around speed, response time, load time and poor scalability. Speed is often one of the most important attributes of an application. A slow running application will lose potential users. Performance testing is done to make sure an app runs fast enough to keep a user's attention and interest. Take a look at the following list of common performance problems and notice how speed is a common factor in many of them:

- **Long Load time** - Load time is normally the initial time it takes an application to start. This should generally be kept to a minimum. While some applications are impossible to make load in under a minute, Load time should be kept under a few seconds if possible.

- **Poor response time** - Response time is the time it takes from when a user inputs data into the application until the application outputs a response to that input. Generally this should be very quick. Again if a user has to wait too long, they lose interest.

- **Poor scalability** - A software product suffers from poor scalability when it cannot handle the expected number of users or when it does not accommodate a wide enough range of users. Load testing should be done to be certain the application can handle the anticipated number of users.

- **Bottlenecking** - Bottlenecks are obstructions in system which degrade overall system performance. Bottlenecking is when either coding errors or hardware issues cause a decrease of throughput under certain loads. Bottlenecking is often caused by one faulty section of code. The key to fixing a bottlenecking issue is to find the section of code that is causing the slow down and try to fix it there. Bottle necking is generally fixed by either fixing poor running processes or adding additional Hardware. Some **common performance bottlenecks** are

  - CPU utilization

  - Memory utilization

  - Network utilization

  - Operating System limitations

  - Disk usage

Performance Testing Process

The methodology adopted for performance testing can vary widely but the objective for performance tests remain the same. It can help demonstrate that your software system meets certain pre-defined performance criteria. Or it can help compare performance of two software systems. It can also help identify parts of your software system which degrade its performance.

Below is a generic performance testing process

1. **Identify your testing environment** - Know your physical test environment, production environment and what testing tools are available. Understand details of the hardware, software and network configurations used during testing before you begin the testing process. It will help testers create more efficient tests. It will also help identify possible challenges that testers may encounter during the performance testing procedures.

2. **Identify the performance acceptance criteria -** This includes goals and constraints for throughput, response times and resource allocation. It is also necessary to identify project success criteria outside of these goals and constraints. Testers should be empowered to set performance criteria and goals because often the project specifications will not include a wide enough variety of performance benchmarks. Sometimes there may be none at all. When possible finding a similar application to compare to is a good way to set performance goals.

3. **Plan & design performance tests -** Determine how usage is likely to vary amongst end users and identify key scenarios to test for all possible use cases. It is necessary to simulate a variety of end users, plan performance test data and outline what metrics will be gathered.

4. **Configuring the test environment -** Prepare the testing environment before execution. Also, arrange tools and other resources.

5. **Implement test design -** Create the performance tests according to your test design.

6. **Run the tests -** Execute and monitor the tests.

7. **Analyze, tune and retest** - Consolidate, analyze and share test results. Then fine tune and test again to see if there is an improvement or decrease in performance. Since improvements generally grow smaller with each retest, stop when bottlenecking is caused by the CPU. Then you may have the consider option of increasing CPU power.

Performance Parameters Monitored

The basic parameters monitored during performance testing include:

- **Processor Usage -** amount of time processor spends executing non-idle threads.

- **Memory use -** amount of physical memory available to processes on a computer.

- **Disk time -** amount of time disk is busy executing a read or write request.

- **Bandwidth -** shows the bits per second used by a network interface.

- **Private bytes** - number of bytes a process has allocated that can't be shared amongst other processes. These are used to measure memory leaks and usage.

- **Committed memory** - amount of virtual memory used.

- **Memory pages/second** - number of pages written to or read from the disk in order to resolve hard page faults. Hard page faults are when code not from the current working set is called up from elsewhere and retrieved from a disk.

- **Page faults/second** - the overall rate in which fault pages are processed by the processor. This again occurs when a process requires code from outside its working set.

- **CPU interrupts per second** - is the avg. number of hardware interrupts a processor is receiving and processing each second.

- **Disk queue length** - is the avg. no. of read and write requests queued for the selected disk during a sample interval.

- **Network output queue length** - length of the output packet queue in packets. Anything more than two means a delay and bottlenecking needs to be stopped.

- **Network bytes total per second** - rate which bytes are sent and received on the interface including framing characters.

- **Response time** - time from when a user enters a request until the first character of the response is received.

- **Throughput** - rate a computer or network receives requests per second.

- **Amount of connection pooling** - the number of user requests that are met by pooled connections. The more requests met by connections in the pool, the better the performance will be.

- **Maximum active sessions** - the maximum number of sessions that can be active at once.

- **Hit ratios** - This has to do with the number of **SQL** statements that are handled by cached data instead of expensive I/O operations. This is a good place to start for solving bottlenecking issues.

- **Hits per second** - the no. of hits on a web server during each second of a load test.

- **Rollback segment** - the amount of data that can rollback at any point in time.

- **Database locks** - locking of tables and databases needs to be monitored and carefully tuned.

- **Top waits** - are monitored to determine what wait times can be cut down when dealing with the how fast data is retrieved from memory

- **Thread counts** - An applications health can be measured by the no. of threads that are running and currently active.

- **Garbage collection** - It has to do with returning unused memory back to the system. Garbage collection needs to be monitored for efficiency.

Performance Test Tools

There are a wide variety of performance testing tools available in market. The tool you choose for testing will depend on many factors such as types of protocol supported , license cost , hardware requirements , platform support etc. Below is a list of popularly used testing tools.

- **HP LoadRunner** - is the most popular performance testing tools on the market today. This tool is capable of simulating hundreds of thousands of users, putting applications under real life loads to determine their behavior under expected loads. **Loadrunner** features a virtual user generator which simulates the actions of live human users.

- **LoadView Testing** - test your infrastructure at any scale. From small targeted tests to millions of users, find performance bottlenecks and adjust your capacity plan accordingly. LoadView offers on-demand, 100% cloud based load testing. Test user experience with real browsers, for a complete performance picture.

- **HTTP Load** - a throughput testing tool aimed at testing web servers by running several http or https fetches simultaneously to determine how a server handles the workload.

- **Jmeter** - one of the leading tools used for load testing of web and application servers.

Summary

Performance testing is necessary before marketing any software product. It ensures customer satisfaction & protects investor's investment against product failure. Costs of performance testing are usually more than made up for with improved customer satisfaction, loyalty and retention.

Load Testing

What is Load Testing?

Load testing is a kind of performance testing which determines a system's performance under real-life load conditions. This testing helps determine how the application behaves when multiple users access it simultaneously.

This testing usually identifies -

- The maximum operating capacity of an application

- Determine whether current infrastructure is sufficient to run the application

- Sustainability of application with respect to peak user load

- Number of concurrent users that an application can support, and scalability to allow more users to access it.

It is a type of non-functional testing. Load testing is commonly used for the Client/Server, Web based applications - both Intranet and Internet.

Need of Load Testing:

Some extremely popular sites have suffered serious downtimes when they get massive traffic volumes. E-commerce websites invest heavily in advertising campaigns, but not in Load Testing to ensure optimal system performance, when that marketing brings in traffic.

Consider the following examples

- Popular toy store Toysrus.com, could not handle the increased traffic generated by their advertising campaign resulting in loss of both marketing dollars, and potential toy sales.

- An Airline website was not able to handle 10000+ users during a festival offer.

- Encyclopedia Britannica declared free access to their online database as a promotional offer. They were not able to keep up with the onslaught of traffic for weeks.

Many sites suffer delayed load times when they encounter heavy traffic. Few Facts -

- Most users click away after 8 seconds' delay in loading a page

- $ 4.4 Billion Lost annually due to poor performance

Why Load Testing?

- Load testing gives confidence in the system & its reliability and performance.

- Load Testing helps identify the bottlenecks in the system under heavy user stress scenarios before they happen in a production environment.

- Load testing gives excellent protection against poor performance and accommodates complementary strategies for performance management and monitoring of a production environment.

Goals of Load Testing:

Loading testing identifies the following problems before moving the application to market or Production:

- Response time for each transaction

- Performance of System components under various loads

- Performance of Database components under different loads

- Network delay between the client and the server

- Software design issues

- Server configuration issues like Web server, application server, database server etc.

- Hardware limitation issues like CPU maximization, memory limitations, network bottleneck, etc.

Load testing will determine whether system needs to be fine-tuned or modification of hardware and software is required to improve performance.

Environment needs to be setup before starting the load testing:

Hardware Platform	Software Configuration
<ul><li>Server Machines</li><li>Processors</li><li>Memory</li><li>Disk Storage</li><li>Load Machines configuration</li><li>Network configuration</li></ul>	<ul><li>Operating System</li><li>Server Software</li></ul>

Prerequisites of load testing:

The chief metric for load testing is response time. Before you begin load testing, you must determine -

- Whether the response time is already measured and compared - Quantitative

- Whether the response time is applicable to the business process - Relevant

- Whether the response time is justifiable - Realistic

- Whether the response time is achievable - Achievable

- Whether the response time is measurable using a tool or stopwatch - Measurable

Strategies of load Testing:

There are many numbers of ways to perform load testing. Following are a few load testing strategies-

Load Testing Process:

The load testing process can be briefly described as below -

1. Create a dedicated test environment for load testing

2. Determine the following

3. Load Test Scenarios

4. Determine load testing transactions for an application

    o Prepare Data for each transaction

    o Number of Users accessing the system need to be predicted

    o Determine connection speeds. Some users may be connected via leased lines while others may use dial-up

    o Determine different browsers and operating systems used by the users

    o Configuration of all the servers like web, application and DB Servers

5. Test Scenario execution and monitoring. Collecting various metrics

6. Analyze the results. Make recommendations

7. Fin-tune the System

8. Re-test

Difference between Load and Stress testing:

Load Testing	Stress Testing
Load testing identifies the bottlenecks in the system under various workloads and checks how the system reacts when the load is gradually increased	Stress testing determines the breaking point of the system to reveal the maximum point after which it breaks.

Difference between Functional and Load Testing:

Functional Testing	Load Testing
Results of functional tests are easily predictable as we have proper steps and preconditions defined	Results of load tests are unpredictable
Results of functional tests vary slightly	Load test results vary drastically
Frequency of executing functional testing will be high	Frequency of executing load testing will be low
Results of functional tests are dependent on the test data	Load testing depends on the number of users.

Load Testing Tools:

Tools recommended for load testing are:

- WebLOAD
- LoadView
- **Loadrunner**
- Astra Load Test
- Studio, Rational Site Load
- Silk Performer
- **Jmeter**

WebLOAD, LoadView and **Loadrunner** and are the most

popular load testing tools. Their features are listed below —

WebLOAD:

WebLOAD is an enterprise scale load testing product that supports hundreds of technologies, enterprise applications, network protocols and operating systems. WebLOAD is known for flexibility — it supports many integrations and the scripting lets you run complex test scenarios.

With WebLOAD, you can generate load on premise or in the cloud.

WebLOAD major features include:

- Comprehensive IDE with correlation, parameterization, response validation and native JavaScripting.

- Load Generation Console which generates massive virtual user load — locally and on the cloud, on Windows or Linux, via **AWS** or other cloud providers.

- Analytics Dashboards with over 80 configurable report templates and a web dashboard for collaborative root cause analysis.

LoadView Testing

LoadView is a cloud based load testing platform that offers complete testing flexibility. Test webservers and Web APIs (REST, SOAP, JSON/XML) by generating a sequence of HTTP GET/POST requests. LoadView is also capable of simulating user behavior for web apps, portal logins, shopping carts and web transactions in a real browser.

With LoadView, you can test your infrastructure at any scale. From small targeted tests to millions of users, find performance bottlenecks and adjust your capacity plan accordingly.

LoadView features include:

- 100% managed cloud

- On-demand load tests

- Real browser testing

- Test on 40+ devices with multi-browser support

- Multi-location load testing

Signup for a free trial of **LoadView here**

Load Runner:

Load runner is HP tool used to test the applications under normal and peak load conditions. Load runner generates load by creating virtual users that emulate network traffic. It simulates real time usage like a production environment and gives graphical results.

Advantages and disadvantages of Load testing:

Following are the advantages of Load testing:

- Performance bottlenecks identification before production

- Improves the scalability of the system

- Minimize risk related to system down time

- Reduced costs of failure

- Increase customer satisfaction

Disadvantages of Load testing:

- Need programming knowledge to use load testing tools.

- Tools can be expensive as pricing depends on the number of virtual users supported.

Conclusion:

Load testing typically improves performance bottlenecks, scalability and stability of the application before it is available for production. This testing helps to identify the maximum operating capacity of applications as well as system bottlenecks.

Accessibility Testing

What is accessibility testing?

Accessibility Testing is a subset of usability testing, and it is performed to ensure that the application being tested is usable by people with disabilities like hearing, color blindness, old age and other disadvantaged groups.

People with disabilities use assistive technology which helps them in operating a software product.

- **Speech RecognitionSoftware -** It will convert the spoken word to text , which serves as input to the computer.

- **Screen reader software** - Used to read out the text that is displayed on the screen

- **Screen Magnification Software**- Used to enlarge the monitor and make reading easy for vision-impaired users.

- **Special keyboard** made for the users for easy typing who have motor control difficulties

Why accessibility Testing?

Reason 1: Cater to market for Disabled People.

About 20% of the population has disability issues.

- 1 in 10 people have a sever disability

- 1 in 2 people over 65 have reduced capabilities

Disabilities include blindness, deaf, handicapped, or any disorders in the body.

A software product can cater to this big market, if it's made disabled friendly. Accessibility issues in software can be resolved if Accessibility Testing is made part of normal testing life cycle.

Reason 2: Abide by Accessibility Legislations

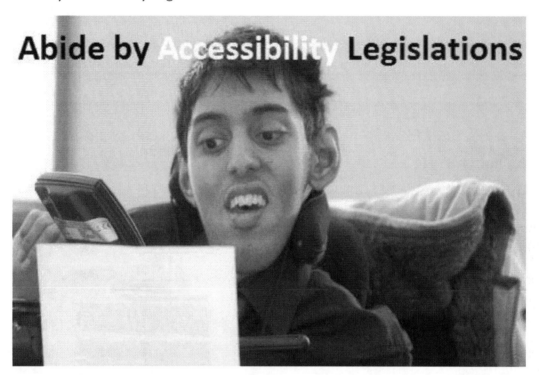

Government agencies all over the world have come out with legalizations, which requires that IT products to be accessible by disabled people.

Following are the legal acts by various governments -

- United States: Americans with Disabilities Act - 1990

- United Kingdom: Disability Discrimination Act - 1995

- Australia: Disability Discrimination Act - 1992

- Ireland : Disability Act of 2005

Accessibility Testing is important to ensure legal compliance.

Reason 3: Avoid Potential Law Suits

In the past, Fortune 500 companies have been sued because their products were not disabled friendly. Here a few prominent cases

- National Federation for the Blind (NFB) vs Amazon (2007)

- Sexton and NFB vs Target (2007)

- NFB Vs AOL settlement (1999)

It's best to create products which support disabled and avoid potential lawsuits.

Which disabilities to support?

Application must support people with disabilities like -

Type of Disability	Disability Description
Vision Disability	• Complete Blindness or Color Blindness or Poor Vision • Visual problems like visual strobe and flashing effect problems
Physical Disability	• Not able to use the mouse or keyboard with one hand. • Poor motor skills like hand movements and muscle slowness
Cognitive disability	• Learning Difficulties or Poor Memory or not able to understand more complex scenarios

Literacy Disability	• Reading Problems
Hearing Disability	• Auditory problems like deafness and hearing impairments • Cannot able to hear or not able to hear clearly

How to do accessibility testing?

Accessibility Testing can be performed in 2 ways, and they are:

1. Manual

2. Automated

Following are the point's needs to be checked for application to be used by all users. This checklist is used for signing off accessibility testing.

1. Whether an application provides keyboard equivalents for all mouse operations and windows?

2. Whether instructions are provided as a part of user documentation or manual? Is it easy to understand and operate the application using the documentation?

3. Whether tabs are ordered logically to ensure smooth navigation?

4. Whether shortcut keys are provided for menus?

5. Whether application supports all operating systems?

6. Whether response time of each screen or page is clearly mentioned so that End Users know how long to wait?

7. Whether all labels are written correctly in the application?

8. Whether color of the application is flexible for all users?

9. Whether images or icons are used appropriately, so it's easily understood by the end users?

10. Whether an application has audio alerts?

11. Whether a user is able to adjust audio or video controls?

12. Whether a user can override default fonts for printing and text displays?

13. Whether user can adjust or disable flashing, rotating or moving displays?

14. Check to ensure that color-coding is never used as the only means of conveying information or indicating an action

15. Whether highlighting is viewable with inverted colors? Testing of color in the application by changing the contrast ratio

16. Whether audio and video related content are properly heard by the disability people ? Test all multimedia pages with no speakers in websites

17. Whether training is provided for users with disabilities that will enable them to become familiar with the software or application?

Accessibility testing may be challenging for testers because they are unfamiliar with disabilities. It is better to work with disabled people who have specific needs to understand their challenges.

There are different way of Testing the Accessibility depending upon the Disability. We will learn all them one by one.

1. **Vision Disability**

OK now let us assume I don't have vision ability. I am completely blind, and I wanted to access XYZ Website. In that case, what is the option???? Cannot I access the XYZ website? What the option do I have? There is one-word option which is termed as **SCREENREADER.** Yeah, you got it right. SCREENREADER. Now, what is this Screen reader? It is a Software which is used for narrating the content on the web. Basically, what is on your website whether it is content, Link, Radio Button, Images, Video, etc. A screen reader will narrate each and everything for me. There are numerous Screen Reader available. I have worked with jaws.

Basically, when you start jaws or any screen reader and then go to the website, then it will narrate you the complete content. For Ex: I have started jaws, and started the browser JAWS will announce that Mozilla Firefox starts page, now if I go to address bar then JAWS will announce that **ADDRESS BAR** and then type **www.google.com** on address bar, jaws will going to explain somewhat like this:-

Address Bar,**w,w,w,period,g,o,o,g,l,e,period,c,o,m. Also, when the page loads completely jaws will again announce Google.Com Home page.**

Now if I go to Google Search, then JAWS will announce that Google search. So it would be easy for a blind person to recognize things in an easy manner.

The point I want to explain here a screen reader will narrate word by word if you enter something or in the text box. Similarly, if there is link it will pronounce it as a link, for Button it will pronounce it as a button. So that a Blind person can easily Identify things.

Now If a website is poorly designed and developed, then it might be possible (it generally happens) that jaws would not be able to narrate correct content which in turn result for inaccessibility for Blind Person.(Say if jaws are narrating a link as a content, then a blind user would never able to know that it's a link and if that would be a crucial one for that website then ????).In that case, it would be a result into a high loss for Website Business.

2) **Visual Impairment**: - There are two categories which I want to be mentioned under visual impairment.

The first one is Color Blindness. Color Blindness means not completely blind but not able to view some specific color properly. Red and Blue are the common colors which people not able to see properly if they do have color blindness. So basically, if I do have a color blindness of red color and I want to use website which is 80% in red then???Would I be comfortable on that website? The answer is No.

So a website should be designed such that a person with color blindness does not have any problem to access that. Take a simple example, for a button which is in Red, to make it accessible if it is outlined with Black, and then it is easy to accessible. Normally Black and white are considered as universal.

POOR VISION DISABILITY

The second thing is a person having poor vision (not clear vision) or having different eyesight problem (there are many eye problem related to the retina, etc.) for accessing any site.

1) In such cases, the best thing to do is avoid small text. Because it would be a great advantage for poorly vision people.

2) Also, people with vision problem would like to zoom text of website to make it comfortable for them. So a website should be designed in such a manner that if enlarging it, its layout is not breakable when zooming the text. Otherwise, it won't be a good impression for them.

Other Disability: In Accessibility Testing for Disabled audience one very major point to consider is Accessing the Website without the use of the mouse. A person should be able to complete access the website the links, buttons, radio buttons, checkboxes, pop-ups, dropdown, all the controls should be completely accessible and operable through the keyboard.

For Example: If I am right handed paralyzed, and I am not comfortable with a mouse or say I don't want to use a mouse then what? In that case, if I am not able to access link or checkboxes on site via keyboard then???? So a website should be completely accessible with Keyboard.

Alternative Text should be there for Images, Audio, Video so that screen reader reads them and will narrate them so that a blind person can easily recognize what the image, audio, the video is all about. In addition, to it, keyboard shortcuts should be there to easily access website and navigation should be available with the keyboard.

Also, the focus should be completely visible. When we are pressing tab, then the user should be able to see where the control is moving. With visible focus, it becomes very easy for a user having poor vision or color blindness to identify the flow of a site and also an ease of access.

User with Hearing Disability (Deaf or hard to listen): The last ones are a person having a disability of Hearing. A deaf person can access the website as he is what able to see the content on the website. But when it comes to audio and video they face difficulties. So in that case, for any Video and Audio, there should be Alt text. Alt text means Alternative text. Suppose there is any Video about how to Book an airline ticket. In that case, the text should be there so that a deaf person can read that and get the idea what the video is all about.

Accessibility Testing Tools:

To make your website more acceptable and user-friendly, it is crucial that it is easily accessible. There are various tools which can check the accessibility of the website. Some of these popular tools are listed below-

AChecker

Accessibility Checker is a web accessibility evaluation tool. By entering web page URL or by uploading its HTML file web accessibility can be examined. It is a free tool that gives the choice to choose report format. AChecker enables user to create accessibility guidelines.

- It is used for accessibility checking

- Mark-up validation option to validate your HTML while reviewing accessibility

- CSS validation option to validate your stylesheets and inline styles while reviewing accessibility

- For instant review of the HTML surrounding places where accessibility problems are identified, you can display the source code

- Using the REST protocol developers can query AChecker from within their web applications

- Apart from all this features, you can also manage users and groups, check management, guideline management, language management and so on.

Wave

Wave is a free web accessibility tool created by WEBAIM. It is used to validate the web page manually for various aspects of accessibility. This tool can be used to check the intranet, pass-word protected, dynamically generated, or sensitive web pages. Major functions of Web Accessibility Toolbar includes identifying components of a webpage, providing access to alternative view of page content and facilitating the use of third party online applications. It ensures 100% private and secure accessibility reporting

TAW

TAW is the online tool for determining accessibility of your web. This tool analyzes the web site in accordance with W3C web accessibility guidelines and shows accessibilities issues. Web accessibility test issues are categorized into priority 1, priority 2 and priority 3. The interesting feature of TAW is the ability to generate subsets of WCAG 1.0 to test against. In TAW tool, you can either choose to test a single page or multiple pages by "spider" a site. TAW also enable us to define additional checks via the "User Checking's" dialog box

Accessibility Valet

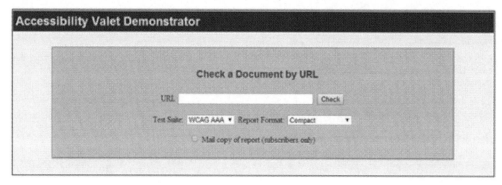

It is a tool that allows you to check web pages against WCAG (Web Content Accessibility Guidelines) compliance. All the HTML reporting options show your markup in a normalized form highlighting deprecated, bogus and valid mark as well as elements that are misplaced. This tool offers various features like

- In-dept reports for developers

- Executive summary for QA and Management

- Meta-data for the semantic web and WWW

- Automatic cleanup and Html to XHtml conversion

- Scripting tools

Accessibility Developer Tools

It is a Chrome extension. It does and accessibility audit. The results of the audit show accessibility rules that are violated by the Page Under Test. The extension has high reviews and is frequently updated

Quick Accessibility Page Tester

Since there are some excellent accessibility toolbars, Quick Page Accessibility Tester is a bookmark that you can click to get a quick analysis of the web page. It will figure out various issues with your page, warns about possible issues and highlight areas on the page which might benefit from ARIA (Accessible Rich Internet Applications).

There are various tools available in the market to perform web accessibility testing given below:

aDesigner

This is a tool developed by IBM which simulates the experience of visually impaired individuals so that the designer can better understand the needs of disabled people and develop applications accordingly.

WebAnywhere

This is a browser based tool that works similarly to the screen readers like Jaws. It assists the readers how to read the web page.

Vischeck

This tool is used to simulate how a web page or an image will be viewed by people affected with color-blindness. This can be done by entering URL or uploading images.

Web accessibility toolbar

WAT is an extension of Internet explorer or Opera that offers web page designers with useful features in the analysis of web page. One best feature is GreyScale feature which helps to find low contrast spots in the design.

Myths of Accessibility Testing:

Following are the Myths of Accessibility Testing:

Myth: Creating Accessible website is expensive

Fact: It is not expensive. Take the timeout to think about accessibility issues in the design stage itself along with basic testing .This will save money as well as rework.

Myth: Changing inaccessible websites to accessible website is time consuming and expensive

It is not necessary to incorporate all the changes at one time. Work on basic needs which are most necessary for disabled users.

Myth: Accessibility is plain and boring

Page Title

Sub-heading

Lorem ipsum dolor sit amet, consectetur adipisicing elit, sed do eiusmod tempor incididunt ut labore et dolore magna aliqua. Ut enim ad minim veniam, quis nostrud exercitation ullamco laboris nisi ut aliquip ex ea commodo consequat. Duis aute irure dolor in reprehenderit in voluptate velit esse cillum dolore eu fugiat nulla pariatur. Excepteur sint occaecat cupidatat non proident, sunt in culpa qui officia deserunt mollit anim id est laborum.

Accessibility doesn't mean text only page

You can make web pages attractive, but it should be designed in such a way that it can be accessible by all users. Also as per W3C web content accessibility guidelines - it strongly discourage the use of text only pages.

Myth: Accessibility if for the Blind and Disabled

Fact Following accessibility guidelines improves the overall usability of the software, which helps regular users as well.

Conclusion

Accessibility testing helps in making your application disabled friendly. If following accessibility guidelines is not possible due to complexity of your web application, build one version of the website for regular users and other for disable

STRESS Testing

What is Stress Testing?

Stress testing is used to test the stability & reliability of the system. This test mainly determines the system on its robustness and error handling under extremely heavy load conditions.

It even tests beyond the normal operating point and evaluates how the system works under those extreme conditions. Stress Testing is done to make sure that the system would not crash under crunch situations.

Stress testing is also known as endurance testing. Under Stress Testing, AUT is be stressed for a short period of time to know its withstanding capacity. Most prominent use **of stress testing is to determine the limit, at which the system or software or hardware breaks**. It also checks whether system demonstrates effective error management under extreme conditions.

The application under testing will be stressed when 5GB data is copied from the website and pasted in notepad. Notepad is under stress and gives 'Not Responded' error message.

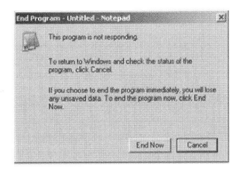

Need for Stress Testing

Consider the following scenarios -

- During festival time, an online shopping site may witness a spike in traffic, or when it announces a sale.

- When a blog is mentioned in a leading newspaper, it experiences a sudden surge in traffic.

It is imperative to perform Stress Testing to accommodate such abnormal traffic spikes. Failure to accommodate this sudden traffic may result in loss of revenue and repute.

Stress testing is also extremely valuable for the following reasons:

- To check whether the system works under abnormal conditions.

- Displaying appropriate error message when the system is under stress.

- System failure under extreme conditions could result in enormous revenue loss

- It is better to be prepared for extreme conditions by executing Stress Testing.

Goals of stress testing:

The goal of stress testing is to analyze the behavior of the system after failure. For stress testing to be successful, system should display appropriate error message while it is under extreme conditions.

To conduct Stress Testing, sometimes, massive data sets may be used which may get lost during Stress Testing. Testers should not lose this security related data while doing stress testing.

The main purpose of stress testing is to make sure that the system recovers after failure which is called as **recoverability**.

Load Testing Vs Stress Testing

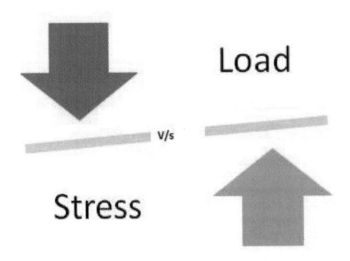

Load Testing	Stress Testing
Load Testing is to test the system behavior under normal workload conditions, and it is just testing or simulating with the actual workload	Stress testing is to test the system behavior under extreme conditions and is carried out till the system failure.
Load testing does not break the system	stress testing tries to break the system by testing with overwhelming data or resources.

Types of Stress Testing:

Following are the types of stress testing and are explained as follows:

Distributed Stress Testing:

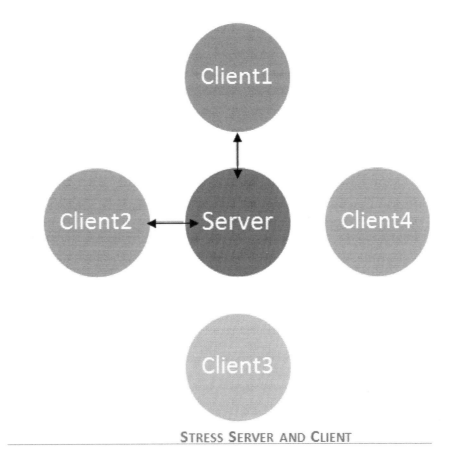

STRESS SERVER AND CLIENT

In distributed client-server systems, testing is done across all clients from the server. The role of stress server is to distribute a set of stress tests to all stress clients and track on the status of the client. After the client contacts the server, server adds the name of the client and starts sending data for testing.

Meanwhile, client machines send signal or heart beat that it is connected with the server. If the server does not receive any signals from the client machine, it needs to be investigated further for debugging. From figure, server can connect with the 2 clients (Client1 and Client2), but it cannot send or receive signal from Client 3 & 4.

Night run is the best option to run these stress testing scenarios. Large server farms, need more efficient method for determining which computers have had stress failures that need to be investigated.

Application Stress Testing:

This testing concentrate on finding defects related to data locking and blocking, network issues and performance bottlenecks in an application.

Transactional Stress Testing:

It does stress testing on one or more transactions between two or more applications. It is used for fine-tuning & optimizing the system.

Systemic Stress Testing:

This is integrated stress testing which can be tested across multiple systems running on the same server. It is used to find defects where one application data blocks another application.

Exploratory Stress Testing:

This is one of the types of stress testing which is used to test the system with unusual parameters or conditions that are unlikely to occur in a real scenario. It is used to find defects around unexpected scenarios like

1. Large number of users logged at the same time

2. If a virus scanner started in all machines simultaneously

3. If Database gone offline when it being accessed from a web site,

4. When a large volume of data is inserted to the database simultaneously

Tools recommended for Stress Testing:

LoadRunner

LoadRunner from HP is a widely-used Load Testing tool. Load Test Results shaped by **Loadrunner** are considered as a benchmark.

Jmeter

Jmeter is an Open Source testing tool. It is a pure **Java** application for stress and performance testing. **Jmeter** is intended to cover types of tests like load, functional, stress, etc. It needs JDK 5 or higher to function.

Stress Tester

This tool provides extensive analysis of the web application performance, provides results in graphical format, and it is extremely easy to use. No high-level scripting is required and gives good return on investment.

Neo load

This is a popular tool available in the market to test the web and **Mobile** applications. This tool can simulate thousands of users in order to evaluate the application performance under load and analyze the response times. It also supports Cloud integrated - performance, load and stress testing. It is easy to use, cost effective, and provides good scalability.

Metrics for stress testing

Metrics help in evaluating a System's performance and generally studied at the end of Stress Test. Commonly used metrics are -

Measuring Scalability & Performance

- Pages per Second :Measures how many pages have been requested / Second

- Throughput: Basic Metric - Response data size/Second

- Rounds: Number of times test scenarios has been planned Versus Number of times client has executed

Application Response

- Hit time: Average time to retrieve an image or a page

- Time to the first byte: Time taken to return the first byte of data or information

- Page Time: Time taken to retrieve all the information in a page

Failures

- Failed Connections: Number of failed connections refused by the client (Weak Signal)

- Failed Rounds: Number of rounds it gets failed

- Failed Hits: Number of failed attempts done by the system (Broken links or unseen images)

Conclusion

Stress testing's objective is to check the system under extreme conditions. It monitors system resources such as Memory, processor, network etc., and checks the ability of the system to recover back to normal status. It checks whether system displays appropriate error messages while under stress.

User Acceptance Testing

User acceptance is a type of testing performed by the Client to certify the system with respect to the requirements that was agreed upon. This testing happens in the final phase of testing before moving the software application to Market or Production environment.

The main purpose of this testing is to validate the end to end business flow. It does NOT focus on the cosmetic errors, Spelling mistakes or System testing. This testing is carried out in separate testing environment with production like data setup. It is a kind of black box testing where two or more end users will be involved.

Who Performs UAT?

- Client

- End users

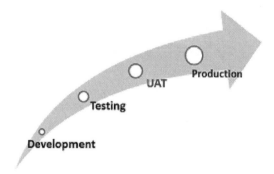

Need of User Acceptance Testing:

Once a software has undergone Unit, Integration and System testing the need of Acceptance Testing may seem redundant. **But Acceptance Testing is required because**

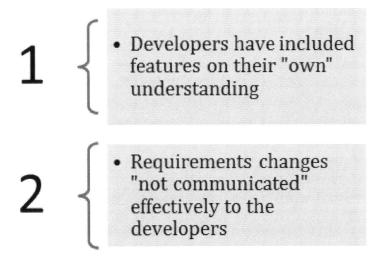

1 — • Developers have included features on their "own" understanding

2 — • Requirements changes "not communicated" effectively to the developers

- Developers code software based on requirements document which is their "own" understanding of the requirements and **may not actually be what the client needs from the software**.

- Requirements changes during the course of the project may not be communicated effectively to the developers.

Acceptance Testing and V-Model

In VModel, User acceptance testing corresponds to the requirement phase of the Software Development life cycle(SDLC).

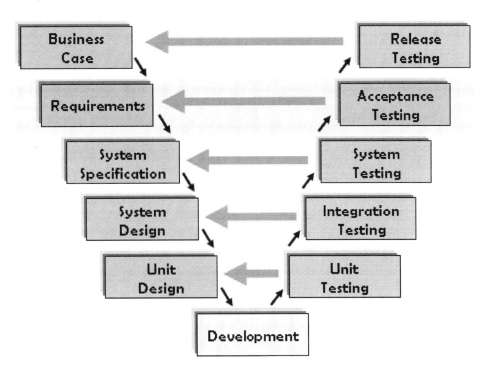

How is UAT Performed
Prerequisites of User Acceptance Testing:

Following are the entry criteria for User Acceptance Testing:

- Business Requirements must be available.

- Application Code should be fully developed

- Unit Testing, Integration Testing & System Testing should be completed

- No Showstoppers, High, Medium defects in System Integration Test Phase -

- Only Cosmetic error are acceptable before UAT

- Regression Testing should be completed with no major defects

- All the reported defects should be fixed and tested before UAT

- Traceability matrix for all testing should be completed

- UAT Environment must be ready

- Sign off mail or communication from System Testing Team that the system is ready for UAT execution

User Acceptance Testing Process:

UAT is done by the intended users of the system or software. This testing usually happens at the client location which is known as Beta Testing. Once Entry criteria for UAT are satisfied, following are the tasks need to be performed by the testers:

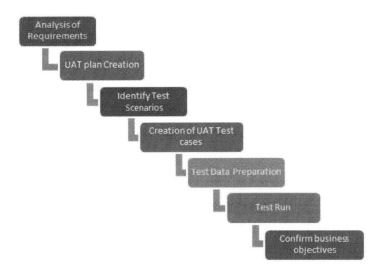

- Analysis of Business Requirements

- Creation of UAT test plan

- Identify Test Scenarios

- Create UAT Test Cases

- Preparation of Test Data(Production like Data)

- Run the Test cases

- Record the Results

- Confirm business objectives

Analysis of Business Requirements

One of the most important activities in the UAT is to identify and develop test scenarios. These test scenarios are derived from the following documents:

- Project Charter

- Business Use Cases

- Process Flow Diagrams

- Business Requirements Document(BRD)

- System Requirements Specification(SRS)

Creation of UAT Plan:

The UAT test plan outlines the strategy that will be used to verify and ensure an application meets its business requirements. It documents entry and **exit criteria for UAT, Test scenarios and test cases approach and timelines of testing**.

Identify Test Scenarios and Test Cases:

Identify the test scenarios with respect to high level business process and create test cases with clear test steps. Test Cases should sufficiently cover most of the UAT scenarios. Business Use cases are input for creating the test cases.

Preparation of Test Data:

It is best advisable to use live data for UAT. Data should be scrambled for privacy and **security** reasons. Tester should be familiar with the data base flow.

Run and record the results:

Execute test cases and report bugs if any. Re-test bugs once fixed. **Test Management** tools can used for execution.

Confirm Business Objectives met:

Business Analysts or UAT Testers needs to send a sign off mail after the UAT testing. After sign-off the product is good to go for production. Deliverables for UAT testing are Test Plan, UAT Scenarios and Test Cases, Test Results and Defect Log

Exit criteria for UAT:

Before moving into production, following needs to be considered:

- No critical defects open

- Business process works satisfactorily

- UAT Sign off meeting with all stakeholders

Qualities of UAT Testers:

UAT Tester should possess good knowledge of the business. He should be independent and think as an **unknown user to the system**. Tester should be Analytical and Lateral thinker and combine all sort of data to make the UAT successful.

Tester or Business Analyst or Subject Matter Experts who understand the business requirements or flows can prepare test and data which are realistic to the business.

Best Practices:

Following points needs to be considered to make UAT Success:

- Prepare UAT plan early in the project life cycle

- Prepare Checklist before the UAT starts

- Conduct Pre-UAT session during System Testing phase itself

- Set the expectation and define the scope of UAT clearly

- Test End to End business flow and avoid system tests

- Test the system or application with real world scenarios and data

- Think as an Unknown user to the system

- Perform Usability Testing

- Conduct Feedback session and meeting before moving to production

UAT Tools

There are several tools in the market used for User acceptance testing and some are listed for reference:

Fitnesse tool : It is **java** tool used as a testing engine. It is easy to create tests and record results in a table. Users of the tool enter the formatted input and tests are created automatically. The tests are then executed and output is returned back to the user.

Watir : It is tool kit used to automate browser based tests during User acceptance testing. Ruby is the programming language used for inter process communication between ruby and Internet explorer.

Some Important points of UAT

- Most of the times in a regular software developing scenarios, UAT is carried out in the QA environment. If there is no staging or UAT environment

- UAT is classified into Beta and Alpha testing but it is not so important when software is developed for a service based industry

- UAT makes more sense when the customer is involved to a greater extent

Conclusion:

UAT is one of the many flavors of testing that has emerged over last twenty five years. With UAT, the client can be sure "What to expect" from the product rather than assuming. The benefit of UAT is that there will be no surprises when the product is released to the market.

Backend Testing

Backend testing is nothing but server side or database testing. The data entered in the front end will be stored in the back-end database. The database may be **SQL** Server, MySQL, Oracle, DB2, etc. The data will be organized in the tables as record, and it is used to support the content of the page. Database testing mainly includes validating

- Schema

- Database tables

- Columns

- Keys and Indexes

- Stored procedures

- Triggers

- Database server validations

- Validating data duplication

In back end testing you are not required to use the GUI; you can directly pass the request through some browser with the parameters required for the function and get a response in some default format. E.g, xml or JSON. You also need to connect to database directly and verify the data using **SQL** queries. Through log files, debugging can be done.

Database or backend testing is important because if it is not done it has some serious complications like deadlock, data corruption, data loss, etc. There are various phases in back-end testing. The first step is to acquire design specification for an **SQL** server. The next step is to test specification design, followed by implementing the tests in this design with **SQL** code.

Types of database testing

The types of database testing includes

- Structural Testing

- Functional Testing

- Non-Functional Testing

Tools used for database testing

Some of the useful tools used for database testing includes

- Data Factory

- Data Generator

- Test Data Generator

- AETG

- TurboData

Advantages for back end testing

- Back end testing is not like a black box testing

- Full control of test coverage and depth

- In early development stage, many bugs can be effectively found

In order to do the back end testing, tester is expected to have strong background in database server and knowledge of structured query language.

Protocol Testing

What is Protocol Testing?

Protocol testing is a generic term used by companies working in the communication industry for testing different protocols in domains of **Switching, Wireless, VoIP, Routing, Switching,** etc.

What is Protocol in a software industry?

When computer communicates with each other, there is a common set of rules and conditions that each computer has to follow. In other words, protocols determine how data are transmitted between computing devices and over networks.

Protocols are classified into two categories **routed protocols** and **a routing protocols**

- **Routed Protocols**: Routed protocols can be used to send the user data from one network to another network. It carries user traffic like e-mails, web-traffic, file transfers, etc. Routed protocols are IP, IPX, and AppleTalk.

- **Routing Protocols**: Routing protocols are network protocols that determine routes for routers. It is only used between routers. For example RIP, IGRP, EIGRP, etc.

In simple terms, **router is like a bus used for transportation while routing protocols are signals on the road.**

Based on the type of communication different protocols are used.

Companies like CISCO, JUNIPER, ALCATEL produce networking devices like routers, modems, wireless access points, etc. that use different protocols for communication, for example, CISCO uses EIGRP, OSPF, etc.

Protocol testing is nothing but checking whether EIGRP (Enhanced Interior Gateway Routing Protocol) or OSPF (Open Shortest Path First) or any other protocol is working as per respective standard.

Types of computer protocols

Types of Protocols	Purpose of Protocols
TCP/IP	It is used to send information in small packets over Internet
UDP/ ICMP	It is used to send small amount of information in data-packets over internet
POP3 and SMTP	It is used for sending and receiving mail
Hypertext Transfer Protocol	It is used to transfer HTML page in encrypted form to provide security to sensitive data
FTP	It is used for transporting files over a network from one node to another

* **TCP/IP**- Transmission Control Protocol/ Internet protocol, **UDP / ICMP**- User Datagram Protocol/Internet Control Message Protocol, **POP3/SMTP**- Post Office Protocol / Simple Mail Transfer Protocol, **HTTP**- Hyper Text Transfer Protocol, **FTP**- File Transfer Protocol

Different types of network Protocols (L2 and L3)

The OSI model has total 7 layer of network communication, in which layer 2 and layer 3 are very crucial.

- **Layer 2**: It is a data link layer. Mac address, Ethernet, Token Ring, and Frame Relay are all examples of Data link layer.

- **Layer 3**: It is a network layer that determines the best available path in the network for communication. IP address is an example of layer3.

Protocol Testing Process

- For protocol testing, you need **protocol analyzer and simulator**

- Protocol analyzer ensures proper decoding along with call and session analysis. While simulator simulates various entities of networking element

- Usually a protocol testing is carried out by DUT (device under test) to other devices like switches and routers and configuring protocol in it

- Thereafter checking the packet structure of the packets send by the devices

- It checks scalability, performance, protocol algorithm etc. of the device by using tools like IxNetworks, Scapy and Wireshark

Testing Types for Protocol Testing

Protocol testing includes testing of functionality, performance, protocol stack, interoperability, etc. During protocol testing basically three checks is done.

- **Correctness**: Do we receive packet X when we expected
- **Latency**: How long does a packet take to transit the system
- **Bandwidth**: How many packets we can send per second

Protocol testing can be segregated into two categories. Stress and Reliability Tests and Functional Tests. Stress and Reliability tests cover load testing, stress testing, performance testing, etc. While functional testing includes negative testing, conformance testing, interoperability testing, etc.

- **Conformance Testing**: The protocols implemented on products are tested for adherence like IEEE, RFC etc.
- **Interoperability Testing**: The interoperability for different vendors are tested. This testing is done after conformance testing is done on the appropriate platform
- **Network feature Testing:** The features on networking products are tested for functionality with reference to the design document. For example features can be port-security on a switch, ACL on a router etc.

Sample Test Cases for Protocol Testing of Network Devices

Here is the sample test case for routers

Test Name	Test Cases
1. One VLAN on One Switch	- Build two different VLANs. Check the visibility between hosts on different VLANs
2. Three Symmatric VLANs on One switch	- Create three different asymmetric VLANs. Check the visibility between hosts
3. Spanning Tree: Root Path Cost Variation	- Test how the Root Path Cost changes after a topology variation
4. Spanning Tree: Port Blocking	- Check how spanning tree protocol avoids formation of cycles in the network, blocking redundant links, in presence of VLANs too
5. Different Root Bridge for	- Show that each MSTI can have different Root Bridge

Different MSTI

6.	Visibility between different STP Regions	• With same VLANs check visibility between different STP regions
7.	Telephone switch Performance	• Generate 1000 telephone calls and check whether the telephone switch still operates or its performance degrades
8.	Negative test for device	• Enter the incorrect key and check the user for authentication. It should not allow user to access
9.	Line speed	• Check the device operating at 10Gbps speed, utilizing all the available bandwidth to handle incoming traffic
10.	Protocol conversation rate	• Track a TCP conversation between two devices and verify that each device engaged in a correct behavior
11.	Response time for session initiation	• Measure the response time of a device to an invite request for session initiation

Tools for Protocol Testing

Lets discuss the most important testing tools used to verify protocols

Scapy For Packet Crafting

Scapy is a powerful interactive packet manipulation program. It enable you to

- Create packets

- Decode packets on the network

- Capture packets and analyze them

- Inject packets into the network

So, basically scapy mainly does two things: **receiving answers and sending packets**. You define the packets, it sends them, receives answers, match requests with answers and returns a list of packet couples and a list of unmatched packets.

It can also handle other things as well like trace-routing, unit tests, attacks or network discovery, developing new protocols, probing, etc.

Scapy enable us to write a **Python** script that allow us to perform a task like sending and receiving packets or sniffing packets. For example, scapy can sniff the data packet by using **Python** script. The command to open the getdit entered in the editor

#gedit scapysniff.py

#!/usr/bin/env python

from scapy.all import*

a= sniff(count=10)

a.nsummary()

save, and change the mode of the file into an executable form

#chmod+x scapysniff.py

./scaotsbuff.py

It will sniff 10 packets and soon as it has sniffed 10 packets it will print the summary. Scapy also as an array of command for sending and receiving packets at the same time

Wireshark Tools For Analysis

Tools used for protocol testing- WireShark . It allows to capture packets in real time and display them in human readable form. It allows you to dig deep into the network traffic and inspect individual packets by using color coding and filters.

Wireshark captures packets that helps to determine when the session is getting established, when the exact data travel was initiated and how much data is sent each time, etc.

Wireshark has a set of rich features which includes

- Thorough inspection of hundreds of protocols, more being added all the time

- Live capture and offline analysis

- Rich VoIP analysis

- Standard three pane packed browser

- Runs on multi-platforms like Windows, Linux, OSX and so on

- Captured network data can be browsed via a GUI

- Decryption support many protocols like IPsec, ISAKMP, SSL/TLS

- Live data can be read from Ethernet, ATM, Bluetooth, USB, token etc.

- Output can be exported to CSV, XML, plain text, etc.

TTCN

TCCN is a standard testing language for defining test scenario and their implementation for protocol testing. A TCCN test suite contains many test cases written in the TTCN programming language and it is used for **testing reactive systems or behavioral testing**.

For example, a coffee vending machine that gives you coffee on inserting a dollar coin but does not respond if anything less than dollar in inserted into it. To program such machines TCCN3 language is used. In order to make coffee machine responds when inserting a coin we have to write TCCN-3 component that behaves as a coffee machine. It allow us to run our test before actual coffee machine is available as a product. Once it is done we will connect the TCCN3 test suite with the external device.

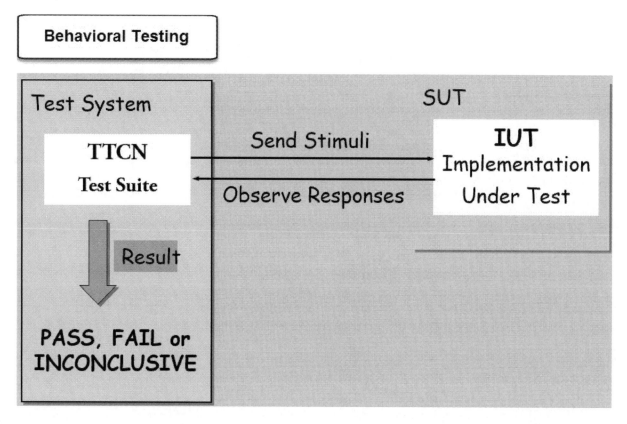

The test system emits stimuli (dollar coin) and receives responses (coffee). The stimuli adapter obtains stimuli from the test system and passes them to the system under test. The response adapter waits for responses of the system under test and passes them to the test system.

TCCN3 can be used in various fields like

- Mobile communications (LTE, WIMAX, 3G etc)

- Broadband technologies (ATM,DSL)

- Middleware Platforms (Webservices, CORBA etc)

- Internet Protocol (SIP, IMS, IPv6)

- Smart Cards

- Automative (AutoSAR, MOST, CAN)

In TCCN we can define

- Test Suites

- Test Cases

- Test Steps

- Declare Variables

- Declare Timers

- Create PDUs etc.

TCCN can be integrated with types systems of other languages like ASN.1, XML , C/ C++ . TCCN3 core language exists in text format apart from other format like tabular, graphical and presentation.

Please share your experiences on Protocol Testing in comments section below

Scrum Testing Beginners

What is Scrum?

Building complex software applications is a difficult task. Scrum methodology comes as a solution for executing such complicated task. It helps development team to focus on all aspects of the product like quality, performance, usability and so on.

Following are Key Features of Scrum-

- Scrum has short fixed schedule of release cycles with adjustable scope known as **sprints** to address rapidly changing development needs. Each release could have multiple sprints. Each Scrum Project could have multiple Release Cycles.

- A repeating sequence of **meetings, events and milestones**

- A practice of **testing and** implementing new requirements, known as **stories**, to make sure some work is released ready after each sprint

Scrum is based on following 3 Pillars-

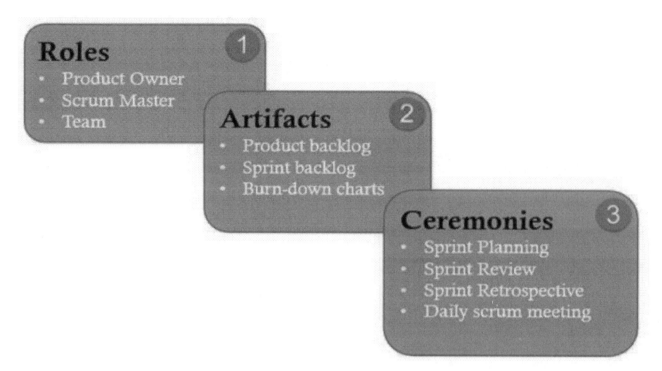

Let's look at the one by one

1. Roles in Scrum

There are three chief roles in Scrum Testing – Product Owner, Scrum Master and The Development Team. Let's study them in detail

Product Owner	Scrum Master	The Team
• He defines features of the product.	• He manages the team and look after the team's productivity	• The team is usually about 5-9 members
• Product Owner decides release date and corresponding features	• He maintains the block list and removes barriers in the development	• It includes developers, designer and sometimes testers, etc.
• They prioritize the features according to the market value and profitability of the product	• He/She coordinates with all roles and functions	• The team organizes and schedule their work on their own
• He is responsible for the profitability of the product	• He/She shields team from external interferences	• Has right to do everything within the boundaries of the project to meet the

		sprint goal
• He can accept or reject work item result	• Invites to the daily scrum, sprint review and planning meetings	• Actively participate in daily ceremonies

2. Scrum Artifacts

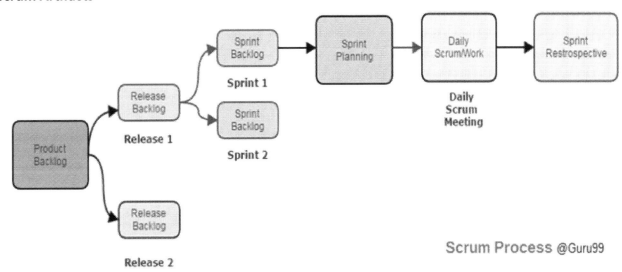

Scrum Process @Guru99

A scrum process includes

- **User stories:** They are short explanation of functionalities of the system under test. Example for Insurance Provider is – "Premium can be paid using the online system."

- **Product Backlog:** It is a collection of user stories captured for a scrum product. **The product owner prepares** and maintains the product backlog. It is prioritized by product owner, and anyone can add to it with approval from the product owner.

- **Release Backlog:** A release is a time frame in which the number of iterations is completed. **The product owner co-ordinates** with the scrum master to decide which stories should be targeted for a release. Stories in the release backlog are targeted to be completed in a release.

- **Sprints:** It is a set period of time to complete the user stories, decided by product owner and developer team, usually 2-4 weeks of time.

- **Sprint Backlog:** It's a set of user stories to be completed in a sprint. During sprint backlog, work is never assigned, and the team signs up for work on their own. It is owned and managed by the team while the estimated work remaining is updated daily. It is the list of task that has to be performed in Sprint

- **Block List:** It is a list of blocks and unmade decisions owned by scrum master and updated daily

- **Burndown chart:** Burn-down chart represents overall progress of the work in progress and work completed throughout the process. It represents in a graph format the stories and features completed

3. Ceremonies (Processes) in Scrum

- **Sprint Planning:** A sprint begins with the team importing stories from the release backlog into the sprint backlog; it is hosted by scrum master. The Testers estimate effort to test the various stories in the Sprint Backlog.

- **Daily Scrum:** It is hosted by scrum master, it last about 15 minutes. During Daily Scrum, the members will discuss the work completed previous day, the planned work for the next day and issues faced during sprint. During daily stand-up meeting team progress is tracked.

- **Sprint Review/ Retrospective:** It is also hosted by scrum master, it last about 2-4 hours and discuss what team has accomplished in the last sprint and what lessons were learned.

Role of Tester in Scrum

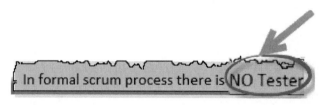

In formal scrum process there is NO Tester

There is no active role of Tester in Scrum Process. Usually, testing is carried out by developer with Unit Test. While product owner is also frequently involved in the testing process during each sprint. **Some Scrum projects do have dedicated test teams depending on the nature & complexity of the project.**

The next question is, what tester do in scrum? Following note will answer

Testing Activities in Scrum

Testers do following activities during the various stages of Scrum-

Sprint Planning

- In sprint planning, tester should pick a user-story from the product backlog that should be tested.

- As a tester, he/she should decide how many hours (Effort Estimation) it should take **to finish** testing for each of selected user stories.

- As a tester, he/she must know what sprint goals are.

- As a tester, contribute to the prioritizing process

Sprint

- Support developers in unit testing

- Test user-story when completed. **Test execution is performed** in a lab where both tester and developer work hand in hand. Defect are logged in Defect Management tool which are tracked on a daily basis. Defects can be conferred and analyzed during scrum meeting. Defects are retested as soon as it is **resolved** and deployed for testing

- As a tester, he/she attends all daily standup meeting to speak up

- As a tester, he/ she can bring any backlog item that cannot be completed in the current sprint and put to the next sprint

- Tester is responsible for developing automation scripts. He schedules automation testing with Continuous Integration (CI) system. Automation receives the importance due to short delivery timelines. Test Automation can be accomplished by utilizing various open source or paid tools available in the market. This proves effective in ensuring that everything that needs to be tested was covered. Sufficient Test coverage can be achieved with a close communication with the team.

- Review CI automation results and send Reports to the stakeholders

- Executing non-functional testing for approved user stories

- Coordinate with customer and product owner to define acceptance criteria for Acceptance Tests

- At the end of the sprint, tester also does acceptance testing(UAT) in some case and confirms testing completeness for the current sprint

Sprint Retrospective

- As a tester, he will figure out what went wrong and what went right in the current sprint

- As a tester, he identifies lesson learned and best practices

Test Reporting

Scrum Test metrics reporting provides transparency and visibility to stakeholders about the project. The metrics that are reported allow team to analyze their progress and plan their future strategy to improve the product. There are two metrics that are frequently used to report.

Burn down chart: Each day, Scrum Master records the estimated remaining work for the sprint. This is nothing but the Burn Down Chart. It is updated daily.

A burndown chart gives a quick overview of the project progress, this chart contains information like total amount of work in the project that must be completed, amount of work completed during each sprint and so on.

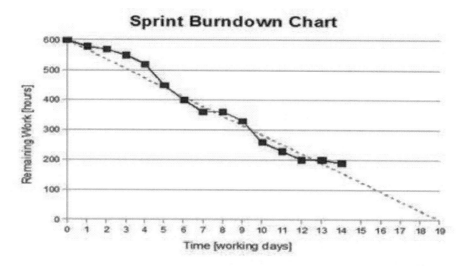

Velocity history graph: The velocity history graph predicts the velocity of the team reached in each sprint. It is a bar graph and represents how teams output has changed over time.

The additional metrics that may be useful are schedule burn, budget burn, theme percent complete, stories completed - stories remaining and so on.

Web Service Testing

What is WebService?

Web Services is the mechanism or the medium of communication through which two applications / machines will exchange the data irrespective of their underline architecture and the technology.

Why is WebService Needed?

In general, software applications are developed to be consumed by the human beings, where a person sends a request to a software service which in-turn returns a response in human readable format.

In the modern era of technology if you want to build a software application you don't need to build each and everything from scratch. There are lots of readymade services available which you can plug into your application and you can start providing those services in your application.

For example you want to display weather forecast information you don't need to collect, process and render the data in your application. You can buy the services from the people who already well-established in processing and publishing such kind of data.

Web services allow us to do these kind of implementations.

As an example, consider the following WebService

http://www.webservicex.net/stockquote.asmx?op=GetQuote

It gives Share Value for a Company.

Let's find share price for Google (Symbol: GOOG)

GetQuote

Get Stock quote for a company Symbol

Test

To test the operation using the HTTP POST protocol, click the 'Invoke' button.

Parameter	Value
symbol:	GOOG

Invoke

The response XML gives the stock price.

This XML file does not appear to have any style information associated with it. The document tree is shown below.

```
▼<string xmlns="http://www.webserviceX.NET/">
    <StockQuotes><Stock><Symbol>GOOG</Symbol><Last>534.03</Last><Date>12/26/2014</Date>
    <Time>4:00pm</Time><Change>+5.26</Change><Open>528.77</Open><High>534.25</High>
    <Low>527.31</Low><Volume>1037774</Volume><MktCap>362.3B</MktCap>
    <PreviousClose>528.77</PreviousClose><PercentageChange>+0.99%</PercentageChange>
    <AnnRange>489.00 - 604.83</AnnRange><Earns>19.002</Earns><P-E>27.83</P-E>
    <Name>Google Inc.</Name></Stock></StockQuotes>
  </string>
```

This WebService can be called by a Software Application using SOAP or HTTP protocol.

Web Services can be implemented in different ways, but the following two are the popular implementations approaches.

1. SOAP (Simple Object Access Protocol)

2. REST (Representational State Transfer architecture)

SOAP

SOAP is a standard protocol defined by the W3C Standard for sending and receiving web service requests and responses.

SOAP uses the **XML format to send and receive the request** and hence the data is platform independent data. SOAP messages are exchanged between the provider applications and receiving application within the SOAP envelops.

As SOAP uses the simple http transport protocol, its messages are not got blocked by the firewalls.

REST

REST means REpresentational State Transfer; it is an architecture that generally runs over HTTP. The REST style emphasizes the interactions between clients and services, which are enhanced by having a limited number of operations. REST is an alternative to SOAP (Simple Object Access Protocol) and instead of using XML for request REST uses simple URL in some cases. Unlike SOAP, RESTFUL applications uses HTTP build in headers to carry meta-information.

There are various code that REST use to determine whether user has access to API or not like code 200 or 201 indicates successful interaction with response body while 400 indicates a bad request or the request URI does not match the APIs in the system. All API request parameters and method parameters can be sent via either **POST** or **GET** variables.

Rest API supports both XML and JSON format. It is usually preferred for **Mobile** and web apps as it makes app work faster and smoother **There is one more thing one needs to learn**

WSDL

WSDL (Web Services Description Language) is an XML based language which will be used to describe the services offered by a web service.

WSDL describes all the operations offered by the particular web service in the XML format. It also defines how the services can be called, i.e what input value we have to provide and what will be the format of the response it is going to generate for each kind of service.

What is Web Service Testing?

Web Services Testing is testing of Web services and its Protocols like SOAP & REST. To test a Webservice you can

1. Test Manually

2. Create your own Automation Code

3. Use an off-the shelf automation tool like SoapUI.

WebService Testing involves following steps -

1. **Understand the WSDL file**

2. **Determine the operations that particular web service provides**

3. **Determine the XML request format which we need to send**

4. **Determine the response XML format**

5. **Using a tool or writing code to send request and validate the response**

Suppose we want to test a WebService which provides Currency Conversion Facility. It will the current conversion rates between the different countries currency. This service we can use in our applications to convert the values from one currency to the other currency.

Now lets look at above steps

Step 1 to 4: Understading WSDL and determining operations & XML formats

Currency Convertor WSDL file can be seen @
(**http://www.webservicex.net/CurrencyConvertor.asmx?wsdl**) which will give the information
about the Currency Convertor web service methods which it will support, the parameter which we
need pass and the type of parameters... etc

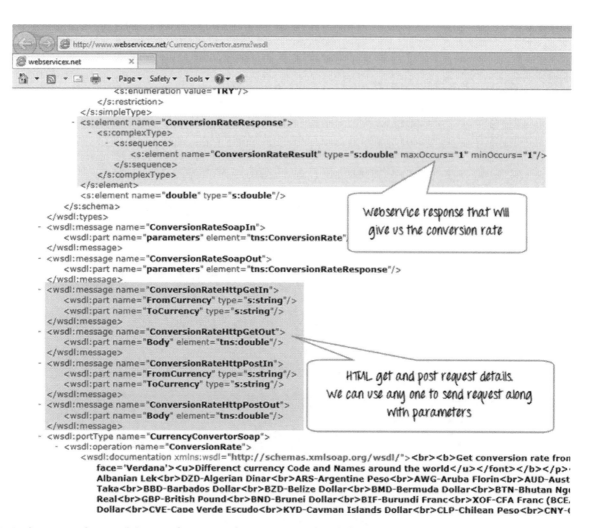

http://www.webservicex.net/CurrencyConvertor.asmx?wsdl

webservicex.net

Page ▾ Safety ▾ Tools ▾

<s:enumeration value="TRY"/>
            </s:restriction>
        </s:simpleType>
        <s:element name="ConversionRateResponse">
            <s:complexType>
                <s:sequence>
                    <s:element name="ConversionRateResult" type="s:double" maxOccurs="1" minOccurs="1"/>
                </s:sequence>
            </s:complexType>
        </s:element>
        <s:element name="double" type="s:double"/>
    </s:schema>
</wsdl:types>
<wsdl:message name="ConversionRateSoapIn">
    <wsdl:part name="parameters" element="tns:ConversionRate"/>
</wsdl:message>
<wsdl:message name="ConversionRateSoapOut">
    <wsdl:part name="parameters" element="tns:ConversionRateResponse"/>
</wsdl:message>
<wsdl:message name="ConversionRateHttpGetIn">
    <wsdl:part name="FromCurrency" type="s:string"/>
    <wsdl:part name="ToCurrency" type="s:string"/>
</wsdl:message>
<wsdl:message name="ConversionRateHttpGetOut">
    <wsdl:part name="Body" element="tns:double"/>
</wsdl:message>
<wsdl:message name="ConversionRateHttpPostIn">
    <wsdl:part name="FromCurrency" type="s:string"/>
    <wsdl:part name="ToCurrency" type="s:string"/>
</wsdl:message>
<wsdl:message name="ConversionRateHttpPostOut">
    <wsdl:part name="Body" element="tns:double"/>
</wsdl:message>
<wsdl:portType name="CurrencyConvertorSoap">
    <wsdl:operation name="ConversionRate">
        <wsdl:documentation xmlns:wsdl="http://schemas.xmlsoap.org/wsdl/">
<b>Get conversion rate from
        face='Verdana'><u>Differenct currency Code and Names around the world</u></font></b></p>
        Albanian Lek
DZD-Algerian Dinar
ARS-Argentine Peso
AWG-Aruba Florin
AUD-Aust
        Taka
BBD-Barbados Dollar
BZD-Belize Dollar
BMD-Bermuda Dollar
BTN-Bhutan Ng
        Real
GBP-British Pound
BND-Brunei Dollar
BIF-Burundi Franc
XOF-CFA Franc (BCE,
        Dollar
CVE-Cape Verde Escudo
KYD-Cayman Islands Dollar
CLP-Chilean Peso
CNY-(

Handwritten note: webservice response that will give us the conversion rate

Handwritten note: HTML get and post request details. We can use any one to send request along with parameters

Step 5: Using a tool or writing code to send request and validate the response

There are lots of tools available to test web services. SoapUI is one of the popular tool which will help us to test the web services. In fact you can use the any programing language which is capable of sending the XML request to the web service provider application over the http and able to parse and validate the response XML against the expected result. In our case, we will test the WebService

1. Using Java

2. Using SoapUI

PART 1) WebService Testing Using Apache Axis2 API (Java).

Generally web service takes the request and sends the response in the XML format.

Apache Axis2 API project is a **Java** implementation API, which will be used to create the Web services for both server side (service provider) and client side (service consumer).

Axis2 is capable of sending SOAP messages and Receives & Processes the SOAP messages. We can write a small Java program using the API to create the web service. Axis2 will generate the WSDL from Java program which will be used to communicate the services offered by the web service. We can use the same Axis2 to generate the Java class (stub) from WSDL file which we can use as a client program to generate the web service request, to send the request to the service end point and to process the response.

1. Basically we will create a simple Java program in which we will instantiate the stub class.

2. Using the stub we will invoke the request method by passing all the required information.

3. Stub program will convert that request into XML request format and sends it the service end point which will read the request and processes the request and sends the response in XML format.

4. The XML response will be converted into Java class by stub and returned to the actual program.

Let's look at above steps in detail

Step a) Download the axis2 API @ **https://axis.apache.org/axis2/Java/core/download.cgi** & Set the environment variable 'AXIS2_HOME'

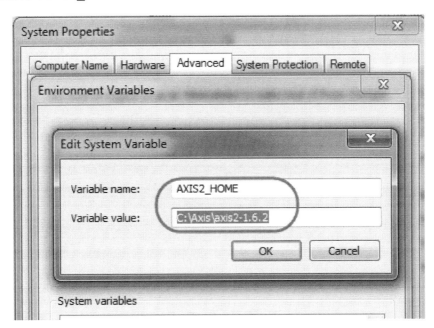

Step b) Create a folder to keep all the generated artifacts

Ex : C:\Axis\Projects\CurrencyConverter

Step c) Open the command prompt and navigate to the folder structure where you want to generate the artifacts and Run the following command which will generate the stubs

%AXIS2_HOME%\bin\WSDL2Java -uri http://www.webservicex.net/CurrencyConvertor.asmx?wsdl -p org.apache.axis2.currencyconvertor -d adb –s

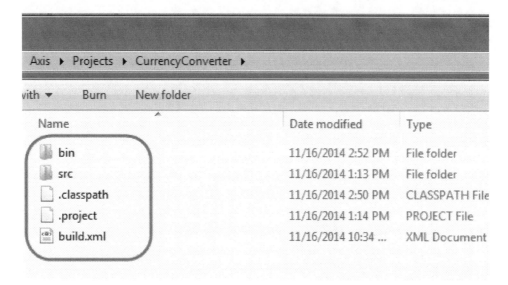

Step d) Once the command is successfully run, you will see the folder with required files.

Step e) Next we have to create the client program, through which we will send the actual request using the generated stubs. Open the eclipse and create the new Java project and select the folder which we have created above.

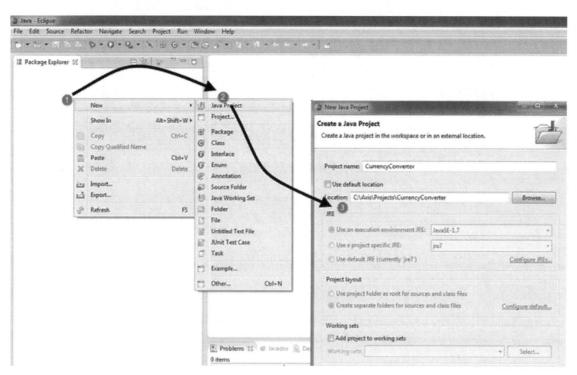

Step f) Add all the axis2 related jars to project build path, which will be there in lib folder of the axis2 software folder

(for ex : C:\Axis\axis2-1.6.2\lib)

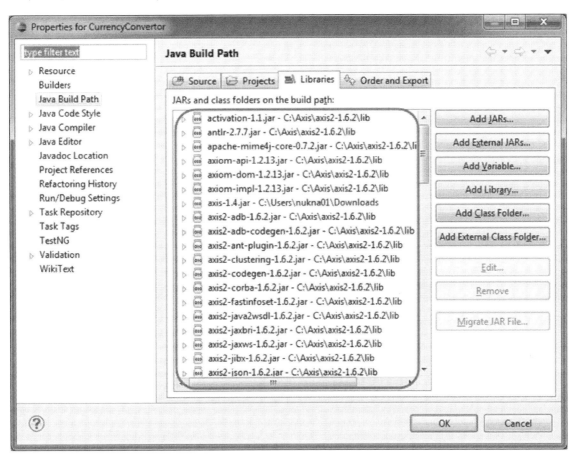

Step g) Create a new Java class (ex : Client.Java) and instantiate stub object. Using the stub object we can call all the supported methods of the particular WebService.

Client.java CurrencyConvertorStub.java

```java
 1  package org.apache.axis2.currencyconvertor;
 2
 3  import org.apache.axis2.currencyconvertor.CurrencyConvertorStub.ConversionRate;
 6
 7  public class Client{
 8      public static void main(java.lang.String args[]){
 9          try{
10
11              //Create the stub object by passing the service end point url
12              CurrencyConvertorStub stub = new CurrencyConvertorStub("http://www.webservicex.net/CurrencyConvertor.asmx");
13
14              //ConversionRate is the class which we have to use mention the from and to currency
15              //ConversionRate object will be the parameter for the conversionRate operation
16              ConversionRate conversionRate =  new ConversionRate();
17              conversionRate.setFromCurrency(Currency.USD);
18              conversionRate.setToCurrency(Currency.INR);
19
20              //Create the ConversionRateResponse object, which is going to be used to catch the response
21              //call the conversionRater service using the stub object
22              ConversionRateResponse conversionRateResponse  = stub.conversionRate(conversionRate);
23
24              //We can use the conversionRateResponse object to retrieve the response of the ConversionRate Service
25              System.out.println("Conversion Rate from INR to USD : " + conversionRateResponse.getConversionRateResult());
26
27          } catch(Exception e){
28              e.printStackTrace();
29          }
30      }
31
32  }
33
34
```

 Problems @ Javadoc Declaration Console

```
<terminated> Client (3) [Java Application] C:\Program Files\Java\jre7\bin\javaw.exe (Nov 16, 2014 10:53:44 PM)
log4j:WARN No appenders could be found for logger (org.apache.axis2.description.AxisOperation).
log4j:WARN Please initialize the log4j system properly.
Conversion Rate from INR to USD : 61.73
```

Client.Java Program

```java
package org.apache.axis2.currencyconvertor;

import org.apache.axis2.currencyconvertor.CurrencyConvertorStub.ConversionRate;

import org.apache.axis2.currencyconvertor.CurrencyConvertorStub.ConversionRateResponse;

import org.apache.axis2.currencyconvertor.CurrencyConvertorStub.Currency;

public class Client {
 public static void main(Java.lang.String args[]) {

 try {

    //Create the stub object by passing the service end point url
    CurrencyConvertorStub stub = new CurrencyConvertorStub("http://www.webservicex.net/CurrencyConvertor.asmx");
    //ConversionRate is the class which we have to use mention the from and to currency
    //ConversionRate object will be the parameter for the conversionRate operation
    ConversionRate conversionRate = new ConversionRate();
    conversionRate.setFromCurrency(Currency.USD);
```

```
conversionRate.setToCurrency(Currency.INR);

//Create the ConversionRateResponse object, which is going to be used to catch the response
//call the conversionRate service using the stub object
ConversionRateResponse conversionRateResponse = stub.conversionRate(conversionRate);

//We can use the conversionRateResponse object to retrieve the response of the ConversionRate Service
System.out.println("Conversion Rate from INR to USD : " + conversionRateResponse.getConversionRateResult());

} catch (Exception e) {
e.printStackTrace();
}
}
}
```

PART 2) Using SoapUI to Test the WebService

In SoapUI

1. Go to File > New Soap Project

2. Enter the project Name and the WSDL URI location

3. Click OK

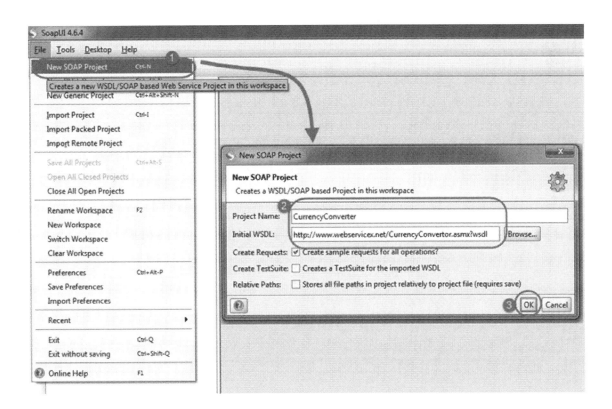

1. Expand the first request and double click on the 'Request1'. It will display the SOAP request in the XML format.

2. Enter the From Currency and To Currency

3. Click on the submit button

4. Response XML will be displayed right side pane.

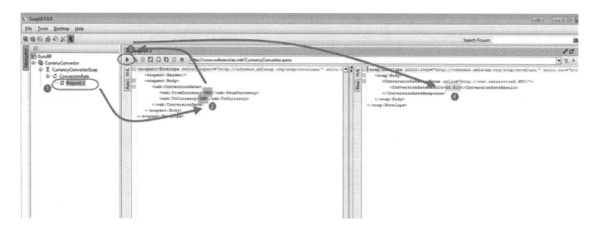

As you may conclude, usage of tools like SoapUI expedites your WebService Testing Effort. Hence SoapUi will be focus of our learning in the succeeding tutorials.

Summary

- Software Applications communicate and exchange data with each other using a WebService

- SOAP and REST are 2 popular protocols to create a WebService

- SOAP supports XML based data exchange

- REST support XML, Json or exchange of data in simple URL.

- WSDL is XML based language which will be used to describe the services offered by a web service. SOAP is defined using WSDL.

- To test WebService you can

  o Create your own code. For instance use Axis2 API for Java

  o Use WebService Test Automation tools like SoapUI

- Automation Tools like SoapUI will jumpstart your testing efforts, will require less coding effort compared to creating your own code using Axis2 API

FAQ

What is Difference between WebService and WebAPI?

Web Service	Web API
• Defined by W3C, all communication & data exchange is based on XML	• Web API communication & data exchange could be XML, JSON or plain data
• It has defined standards – WSDL	• No defined standard
• You cannot compress the data but you can compress the HTML request	• You can compress the data
• Example: SOAP	• Example: REST

Section 4: Testing Different Domains

Banking Domain Application Testing

Banking Applications directly deal with confidential financial data. It is mandatory that all the activities performed by banking software run smoothly and without any error. Banking software perform various functions like transferring and depositing fund, balance inquiry, transaction history, withdrawal and so on. Testing banking application assures that these activities are not only executed well but also remain protected from hackers.

What is Domain in Testing?

Domain is nothing but the industry for which the software testing project is created. When we talk about software project or development, this term is often referred. For example, Insurance domain, Banking domain, Retail Domain, Telecom Domain, etc.

Usually, while developing any specific domain project, domain expert help is sought out. Domain expert are master of the subject, and he may know the inside-out of the product or application.

Why Domain Knowledge Matters?

Domain knowledge is quintessential for testing any software product, and it has its own benefits like

It reduces the training time

It helps in quick defect tracking

It gives good idea on UI features and back-end processing

It gives good hold over workflow, business process and rule

It helps to understand easily the technical terminology

Banking Domain Knowledge - Introduction

Banking domain is huge, and basically it is sub-characterized into two sectors

1. **Traditional banking sector**

2. **Service based banking sector**

Below is the table of the services these two sub-sectors of banking encompass

Traditional banking sector	<ul><li>Core banking</li><li>Corporate banking</li><li>Retail banking</li></ul>
Service based banking sector	<ul><li>Core</li><li>Corporate</li><li>Retail</li><li>Loan</li><li>Trade finance</li></ul>

- Private banking

- Consumer finance

- Islamic banking

- Customer delivery channels/Front end delivery

Based on the scope of your project you may need to test one or all of the above service offerings. Before you begin testing, ensure you have enough background on the service being tested.

Characteristics of a Banking Application

Before you begin testing, it's important to note the standard features expected of any banking application. So that, you can gear your test efforts to achieve these characteristics.

A standard banking application should meet all these characteristics as mentioned below.

- It should support thousands of concurrent user sessions

- A banking application should integrate with other numerous applications like trading accounts, Bill pay utility, credit cards, etc.

- It should process fast and secure transactions

- It should include massive storage system.

- To troubleshoot customer issues it should have high auditing capability

- It should handle complex business workflows

- Need to support users on multiple platforms (Mac, Linux, Unix, Windows)

- It should support users from multiple locations

- It should support multi-lingual users

- It should support users on various payment systems (VISA, AMEX, MasterCard)

- It should support multiple service sectors (Loans, Retail banking etc.)

- Foolproof disaster management mechanism

Test Phases in Testing Banking Applications

For testing banking applications, different stages of testing include

- **Requirement Analysis:** It is done by business analyst; requirements for a particular banking application are gathered and documented

- **Requirement Review:** Quality analysts, business analysts, and development leads are involved in this task. The requirement gathering document is reviewed at this stage, and cross-checked to ensure that it does not affect the workflow

- **Business Requirements Documentation:** Business requirements documents are prepared by quality analysts in which all reviewed business requirements are covered

- **Database Testing:** It is the most important part of bank application testing. This testing is done to ensure data integrity, data loading, data migration, stored procedures, and functions validation, rules testing, etc.

- **Integration Testing:** Under integration testing all components that are developed are integrated and validated

- **Functional Testing:** The usual software testing activities like test case preparation, test case review and test case execution is done during this phase

- **Security Testing:** It ensures that the software does not have any security flaws. During test preparation, QA team needs to include both negative as well as positive test scenarios so as to break into the system and report it before any unauthorized individual access it. While to prevent from hacking, the bank should also implement a multi-layer of access validation like a one-time password. For security testing, automation tools like IBM AppScan and HPWebInspect are used while for manual testing tools like Proxy Sniffer, Paros proxy, HTTP watch, etc. are used

- **Usability Testing:** It ensures that differently able people should be able to use the system as normal user. For example, ATM with hearing and Braille facility for disabled

- **User Acceptance Testing:** It is the final stage of testing done by the end users to ensure the compliance of the application with the real world scenario.

Sample Test Case for Net Banking Login Application

Security is prime for any banking application. Therefore, during test preparation, QA team should include both negative and positive test scenarios in order to sneak into the system and report for any vulnerabilities before any unauthorized individual get access to it. It not only involves writing negative test cases but may also include destructive testing.

Following are generic test cases to check any banking application

Sample test cases
For Admin
• Verify Admin login with valid and Invalid data
• Verify admin login without data
• Verify all admin home links

- Verify admin change password with valid and invalid data

- Verify admin change password without data

- Verify admin change password with existing data

- Verify admin logout

For new Branch

- Create a new branch with valid and invalid data

- Create a new branch without data

- Create a new branch with existing branch data

- Verify reset and cancel option

- Update branch with valid and invalid data

- Update branch without data

- Update branch with existing branch data

- Verify cancel option

- Verify branch deletion with and without dependencies

- Verify branch search option

For New Role

- Create a new role with valid and invalid data

- Create a new role without data

- Verify new role with existing data

- verify role description and role types

- Verify cancel and reset option

- Verify role deletion with and without dependency

- verify links in role details page

For customer & Visitors

- Verify all visitor or customer links

- Verify customers login with valid and invalid data

- Verify customers login without data

- Verify bankers login without data

- Verify bankers login with valid or invalid data

For New users

- Create a new user with valid and invalid data

- Create a new user without data

- Create a new user with existing branch data

- Verify cancel and reset option

- Update user with valid and invalid data

- Update user with existing data

- Verify cancel option

- Verify deletion of the user

Challenges in testing Banking domain & their Mitigation

Challenges tester might face during testing banking domain are

Challenge	Mitigation
• Getting access to production data and replicating it as test data, for testing is challenging	• Ensure that test data meets regulatory compliances requirements and guidelines • Maintain the data confidentiality by following techniques like data masking, synthetic test data, testing system integration, etc.
• The biggest challenge in testing banking system is during the migration of the system from the old system to the new system like testing of all the routines, procedures and plans. Also how the data will be fetched, uploaded and transferred to the new system after migration	• Ensure Data Migration Testing is complete • Ensure Regression Test cases are executed on old and new systems, and the results match.
• There may be the cases where requirements are not documented well and may lead to functional gaps in test plan • Many non-functional requirements are not fully documented, and testers do not know whether to test it or not	• The test should participate in the project right from Requirement Analysis phases and should actively review the Business Requirements
• The most important point is to check whether the said system follows the desired policies and	• Compliance or Regulatory Policies testing must be done

procedures

- The scope and the timelines increases as banking application are integrated with other application like internet or **Mobile** banking

- Ensure Time budget for Integration testing is accounted if your banking application has many external interfaces

Summary

Banking domain is the most vulnerable area for cyber-theft, and safeguarding the software requires precise testing. This tutorial gives a clear idea of what it takes for banking domain testing and how important it is. One must understand that -

- Majority of banking software are developed on **Mainframe** and **Unix**

- Testing helps to lessen possible glitches encounter during software development

- Proper testing and compliance to industry standards, save companies from penalties

- Good practices help develop good results, reputation and more business for companies

- Both manual and automated testing have respective merits and usability

Ecommerce Applications

Setting up an E-commerce system is a complex process and subject to many market specific variables. To maintain the integrity of the E commerce system, testing becomes compulsory. It helps in the prevention of errors and adds value to the product by ensuring conformity to client requirements.

The objective of testing is to ensure

- Software reliability

- Software quality

- System Assurance

- Optimum performance and capacity utilization

Testing E-commerce Applications

Types of Testing for E-commerce System

Common type of testing included into e commerce system are

Sr.#	Type of Testing	Testing Process
1	Browser compatibility	<ul><li>Lack of support for early browsers</li><li>Browser specific extensions</li><li>Browser testing should cover main platforms (Linux, Windows, Mac etc.)</li></ul>
2	Page display	<ul><li>Incorrect display of pages</li><li>Runtime error messages</li><li>Poor page download time</li><li>Dead hyperlink, plugin dependency, font sizing, etc.</li></ul>
3	Session Management	<ul><li>Session expiration</li><li>Session storage</li></ul>
4	Usability	<ul><li>Non-intuitive design</li><li>Poor site navigation</li><li>Catalog navigation</li><li>Lack of help-support</li></ul>
5	Content Analysis	<ul><li>Misleading, offensive and litigious content</li></ul>

		• Royalty free images and copyright infringement
		• Personalization functionality
		• Availability 24/7
6	Availability	• Denial of service attacks
		• Unacceptable levels of unavailability
7	Back-up and Recovery	• Failure or fall over recovery
		• Backup failure
		• Fault tolerance
8	Transactions	• Transaction Integrity
		• Throughput
		• Auditing
9	Shopping order processing and purchasing	• Shopping cart functionality
		• Order processing
		• Payment processing
		• Order tracking
10	Internationalization	• Language support
		• Language display
		• Cultural sensitivity
		• Regional Accounting
11	Operational business procedures	• How well e-procedure copes
		• Observe for bottlenecks
12	System Integration	• Data Interface format
		• Interface frequency and activation

		•	Updates
		•	Interface volume capacity
		•	Integrated performance
13	Performance	•	Performance bottlenecks
		•	Load handling
		•	Scalability analysis
14	Login and Security	•	Login capability
		•	Penetration and access control
		•	Insecure information transmission
		•	Web attacks
		•	Computer viruses
		•	Digital signatures

Performance testing- a top priority in E-commerce

Just delay about 250 milliseconds of a page load time, is what keeps your customer going to your competitor. Retail giant Walmart overhaul their site speed and noticed an increase of 2% in visitor's conversion rate and revenue by 1%.

Performance of your site depends on this factors

- **Throughput**
  - Request per second
  - Transactions per minute
  - Executions per click

- **Response Time**
  - Duration of a task
  - Seconds per click
  - Page Load
  - DNS Lookup
  - Length of time between click and seeing page

Useful Tools for Mapping E-commerce Site

- **Concept Feedback**: Post your website and get feedback from experts

- **ClickHeat**: It shows the most clicked and unclicked zones of sites by visitors

- **FiveSecondTest**: This tool ensures that your message is communicated as effectively as possible, in just five seconds it tells what a person recalls about your website design

- **Feedback Army**: For your e commerce site it start a usability test by submitting questions about your site and receiving 10 responses from reviewers

- **Feng-GUI**: It simulates the human vision during first five seconds and predicts what a real human would most likely look at

- **Optimizely**: It enables you to test track, clicks, conversions or anything else that matters to e-commerce business

Challenges of E-commerce Testing

- Compliance with security guidelines to safeguard customer data and identity

- Compliance with accessibility standards to support multi-lingual markets and business regions

- End to end testing and test management for large e-commerce transformation programs

- Scalability and reliability of applications

- Compliance with accessibility standards to support multi-lingual markets and business regions

Insurance Application Testing

Insurance Companies rely heavily on Software to run their business. Software Systems helps them to deal with various insurance activities like developing standard policy forms, handling billing process, managing customer's data, rendering quality services to the customer, coordinating between branches and so on.

Though this software is designed to meet the customer's expectations, its durability and consistency needs to be tested before its actual deployment. Software testing assures the quality of the insurance software by identifying bugs before go-live.

What is Domain in Testing?

Domain is nothing but the industry for which the software testing project is created. When we talk about software project or development, this term is often referred. For example, Insurance domain, Banking domain, Retail Domain, Health Care Domain, etc.

Usually, while developing any specific domain project, domain expert help is sought out. Domain expert are master of the subject, and he may know the inside-out of the product or application.

Why Insurance Domain Knowledge Matters?

Domain knowledge is quintessential for testing any software product, and it has its own benefits like

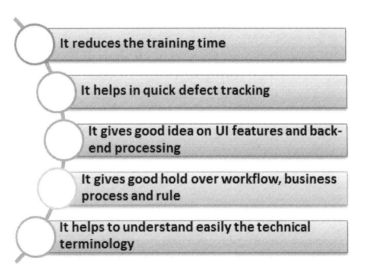

- It reduces the training time
- It helps in quick defect tracking
- It gives good idea on UI features and back-end processing
- It gives good hold over workflow, business process and rule
- It helps to understand easily the technical terminology

What is Insurance? Type of Insurance

Insurance is defined as the equitable transfer of the risk of a loss from one entity to another in exchange for payment. Insurance Company, which sells the policy is referred as INSURER while the person or company who avails the policy is called the INSURED.

Insurance policies are usually classified into two categories, and insurer buy these policies as per their requirement and budget.

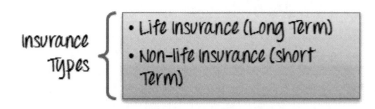

However, there are other types of insurance that falls under these categories

- Unemployment insurance

- Social Security

- Workers Compensation

What is Premium? How is Premium calculated?

Premium is defined as the amount to be charged for a certain amount of insurance coverage or policy the insured has bought.

Premium for the insurance is determined by on the basis of two factors

- The frequency of claims

- The Severity of claims (Cost of each claim)

For example, we will see how insurance system works,

Suppose an insurance company provides insurance to all houses in a village

Home Insurance	Amount
Total number of house in village	= 1000
Value of each house	= $ 800
Contribution of each house owner as premium	= $ 8

Total Premium Collected	= $8000

Statistically, it has calculated that in case of fire a maximum of 10 houses are burnt which it need to compensate.

So incase, of fire, it will have to pay 10 house $800 which comes $8000 equal to the premium it collected.

The risk of 10 house owners is spread over 1000 house owner in the village hence reducing the burden on any one of the owner.

In case of no fire in a particular year, the entire sum goes to its profit while if more than 10 houses burn the insurer will incur a loss.

Testing required in different process area of Insurance

Testing can mitigate the risk of business disruption during and after deployment of software. There are many branches of an insurance company that requires testing.

- Policy Administration Systems
- Claim Management Systems
- Distribution Management Systems
- Investment Management Systems
- Third party Administration Systems
- Risk Management Solutions
- Regulatory and Compliance
- Actuarial Systems (Valuation & Pricing)

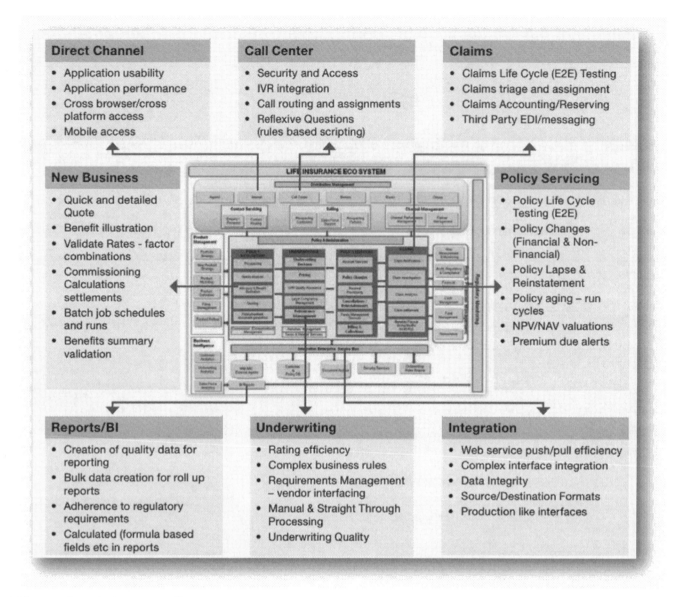

Direct Channel
- Application usability
- Application performance
- Cross browser/cross platform access
- Mobile access

Call Center
- Security and Access
- IVR integration
- Call routing and assignments
- Reflexive Questions (rules based scripting)

Claims
- Claims Life Cycle (E2E) Testing
- Claims triage and assignment
- Claims Accounting/Reserving
- Third Party EDI/messaging

New Business
- Quick and detailed Quote
- Benefit illustration
- Validate Rates - factor combinations
- Commissioning Calculations settlements
- Batch job schedules and runs
- Benefits summary validation

Policy Servicing
- Policy Life Cycle Testing (E2E)
- Policy Changes (Financial & Non-Financial)
- Policy Lapse & Reinstatement
- Policy aging – run cycles
- NPV/NAV valuations
- Premium due alerts

Reports/BI
- Creation of quality data for reporting
- Bulk data creation for roll up reports
- Adherence to regulatory requirements
- Calculated (formula based fields etc in reports

Underwriting
- Rating efficiency
- Complex business rules
- Requirements Management – vendor interfacing
- Manual & Straight Through Processing
- Underwriting Quality

Integration
- Web service push/pull efficiency
- Complex interface integration
- Data Integrity
- Source/Destination Formats
- Production like interfaces

What to Test in Insurance?

The insurance sector is a network of small units that deals directly or indirectly with processing claims. For smooth functioning of an insurance company, it is necessary that each of this unit is tested rigorously before it is sync together to deliver the desired outcome. The testing includes

• **Call Center**	• IVR integration testing
	• Call routing and assignment
	• Security and access
	• Reflexive Questions
• **Policy Serving**	• Policy life cycle testing
	• Financial and Non-financial policy changes

- Policy lapse and Re-instatement

- Policy aging-run cycles

- Premium due alerts

- Valuation of NPV/NAV

- **Claims**
  - Claims triage and assignment

  - Testing claims life cycle

  - Claims accounting/reserving

  - Third party EDI/messaging

- **Direct channel**
  - Mobile access

  - Cross browser/cross platform accessibility

  - Application performance

  - Usability of application

- **Reports/BI**
  - Behaving to regulatory requirements

  - Generate quality data for reporting

  - Create bulk data for roll-up reports

  - Testing formula based fields in reports

- **Underwriting**
  - Underwriting quality

  - Manual and Straight through processing

  - Complex business rules

  - Rating efficiency

  - Requirements Management (Vendor Interfacing)

- **Integration**
  - Data integration

  - Complex interface integration

  - Source/Destination formats

- Production like interface
- Web service pull/push efficiency

- **New Business**
  - Validate rates-factor combinations
  - Batch job schedules and runs
  - Commissioning calculations settlements
  - Quick and detailed quote
  - Benefit illustration
  - Benefit summary validation
  - Quick and detailed quote

Sample Test Case for Insurance Application Testing

Sr#	Test Cases for Insurance Application
1	Validate claims rule
2	Ensure that claim can occur to the maximum and minimum payment
3	Verify data is transferred accurately to all sub-systems including accounts and reporting.
4	Check that the claims can be processed via all channels example web, mobile, calls, etc
5	Test for 100% coverage and accuracy in calculations determining premium rates
6	Make sure formula for calculating dividend and paid up values gives correct value
7	Verify surrender values are calculated as per the policy requirement
8	Verify fiduciary details and bookkeeping requirements

9	Test complex scenarios for policy lapse and revivals
10	Test various conditions for non-forfeiture value
11	Test scenarios for policy termination
12	Verify general ledger account behave same as to reconcile with subsidiary ledger
13	Test calculation of net liability for valuation
14	Test conditions for extended term insurance
15	Verify policy for a non-forfeiture option
16	Check different insurance product term behaves as expected
17	Verify premium value as per product plan
18	Test automatic messaging system to inform customer about new products
19	Validate all the data entered by users as it progresses through the workflow to trigger warnings, compliance, notification and other workflow events
20	Verify insurance document template supports the document format like MS-Word
21	Test system for generating invoice automatically and send it to customer through e-mail

Summary

Timely process of the insurance policy and managing client's data is a foremost priority for any insurance company. Their complete dependency on a software solution for handling claims, as well as customers, requires software solution to be precise and accurate. Considering all the key aspects of insurance company's requirement some of the testing strategy and scenarios are represented in this tutorial.

Payment Gateway Testing

A payment gate-way system is an e-commerce application service that **approves**credit card payment for online purchases. Payment gateways safeguard the credit card details by encrypting sensitive information like credit card numbers, account holder details and so on. This information is passed safely between the customer and the merchant and vice versa.

Modern payment gateways also **securely approve** payments via debit cards, electronic bank transfers, cash cards, reward points etc.

Types of Payment Gateway System

- **Hosted Payment Gateway**:

  Hosted payment gateway system direct customer away from e-commerce site to gateway link during payment process. Once the payment is done, it will bring customer back to e-commerce site. For such type of payment you don't need merchant id, example of hosted payment gateway are PayPal, Noche and WorldPay.

- **Shared Payment Gateway**:

  In shared payment gateway, while processing payment customer is directed to payment page and stays on the e-commerce site. Once the payment detail is filled, the payment process proceeds. Since it does not leave the e-commerce site while processing payment, this mode is easy and more preferable, example of shared payment gateway is eWay, Stripe.

Testing Types for Payment Gateway System

Testing for Payment Gateway should include

Functional Testing: It is the act of testing base functionality of the payment gateway. It is to verify whether the application behaves in same way as it is supposed to be like handling orders, calculation, addition of VAT as per the country etc.

Integration: Test integration with your credit card service.

Performance: Identify various performance metrics like highest possible number of users coming through gateways during specific day and converting them to concurrent users

Security: You need to perform a deep security pass for Payment Gateway.

Test Preparation for Testing Payment Gateway

Before you begin testing -

- Collect proper test data for the dummy credit card number for maestro, visa, master etc.

- Collect payment gateway information like Google wallet, Paypal or else

- Collect payment gateway document with error codes

- Understand the session and parameters passed through application and payment gateway

- Understand and test the amount related information passed through query string or variable or session

- Along with payment gateway language check the language of the application

- Under the various settings of payment gateway like currency format, subscriber data collected.

Sample Test Cases for Payment Gateway Testing

Sr#	Test Cases
1	During the payment process try to change the payment gateway language
2	After successful payment, test all the necessary components, whether it is retrieved or not
4	Check what happens if payment gateway stops responding during payment
5	During the payment process check what happens if session ends
6	During the payment process check what happens in back end
7	Check what happens if payment process fails

8	Check the Data-base entries whether they store credit card details or not
9	During payment process check error pages and security pages
10	Check settings of pop-up blocker, and see what happens if pop up blocker is on and off
11	Between payment gateway and application check buffer pages
12	Check on successful payment, a success code is send to the application and a confirmation page is show to the user
13	Verify whether the transaction processes immediately or processing is hand to your bank
14	After successful transaction check if the payment gateway returns to your application
15	Check all format and messages when successful payment process
16	Unless you don't have an authorization receipt from payment gateway, good should not be shipped
17	Inform the owner for any transaction processed through e-mail. Encrypt the content of the mail
18	Check the amount format with currency format
19	Check if each of the payment options are selectable
20	Check if each listed payment option opens the respective payment option according to specification

21	Verify whether the payment gateway defaults to the desired debit/credit card option
22	Verify the default option for debit card shows card selection drop down menu

Things to consider before Buying Gateway Package

- If you have bought a shopping cart package, find out about its compatibility

- If shopping gateway package is due, ask the payment gateway provider for a list of supported applications

- The gateway must offer Address Verification System Protection

- Find out the types of transaction protection being offered

- Check what types of debit or credit cards are accepted by your chosen payment gateway

- Check the transaction fees levied by payment gateway

- Check whether the gateways collect the payment right on the form or direct to another page to complete the purchase

Use the comments section below to contribute more test cases on Payment Gateway Testing

Retail POS Testing

What is POS Testing?

POS Testing is defined as Testing of a Point of Sale Application. A POS or Point Of Sale software is a vital solution for retail businesses to carry out retail transactions effortlessly from anywhere. You must have seen Point of Sale terminal while checking out at your favorite Mall.

The system is more complex than you think and is tightly integrated with other software systems like Warehouse, Inventory, purchase order, supply chain, marketing, merchandise planning etc.

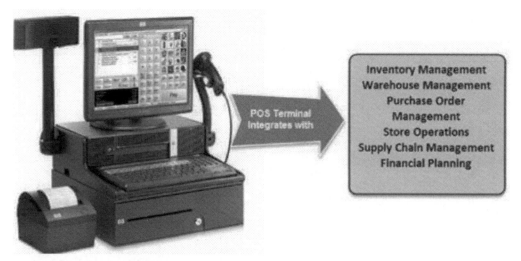

Test Architecture for POS Application

POS test architecture includes three components for testing - POS terminal, store server and enterprise server. Basically it is classified into three levels for testing of POS application.

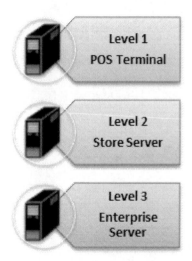

Level 1- (POS Terminal)	Level 2- (Store Server)	Level 3- (Enterprise Server)
• Device and hardware testing (RIFD, Scanner, Printer, Barcode reader) • Interoperability Testing • BI and Analytics Testing • Performance Testing	• Security Testing • BI & Analytics Testing • Disaster recovery Testing • Interface Testing	• Security Testing • BI & Analytics Testing • Disaster Recovery Testing • Interface Testing

Types of Testing for POS system

Testing of POS System can be broken down into two levels

1. Application Level

2. Enterprise Level

Testing Performed At Application Level	Testing Performed At Enterprise Level
• Functionality Testing	• Compliance Testing
• Compatibility Testing	• Performance Testing
• Payment Gateway Testing	• Interoperability Testing
• Report Testing	• Data Migration
	• Mobility

Sample Test Cases for POS used in Retail

To ensure quality of the POS system, proper POS software testing is mandatory. The POS testing spans many things like

Test Scenario	Test Cases
Cashier activity	• Test the entry of items purchased by customer is correct
	• Test discounts are applied correctly
	• Verify store value cards can be used
	• Check petty cash management works as expected
	• Check totals and closings match
	• Check cash drawer loans are handled properly
	• Test the POS system is compatible with peripherals like RFID

Reader, Bar Code Scanner etc.

Payment Gateway Processing	<ul><li>Test the validity of CVV number of Credit Card</li><li>Test swiping of cards from both sides and chips</li><li>Verify that the captured card details are properly encrypted and decrypted</li></ul>
Sales	<ul><li>Check for regular sale process</li><li>Check sales can be processed with debit/credit cards</li><li>Check for loyalty membership purchase</li><li>Check for correct prices are displayed for merchandise purchased</li><li>Test for "0" or null transaction</li><li>Tie UPC or bar codes to vendors</li><li>Test for billing details or shipping details in payment manager</li><li>Test for reference transaction</li><li>Test the print format of the receipt generated</li><li>Verify that the correct code is generated for approved, hold or declined transactions</li></ul>
Return & Exchange scenarios	<ul><li>Make sure the in-house inventory is well integrated with other outlets or supply chain</li><li>Check for exchange or return of an item with cash</li><li>Check whether system responds on exchange or return of an item with credit card</li><li>Check system process the sale with receipt or without receipt</li><li>Verify that system should allow enter bar-code manually incase scanner don't work</li><li>Verify system display both the current amount as well as discount amount on exchange of item if applicable</li></ul>
Performance	<ul><li>Check for speed or time taken to receive a response or send a</li></ul>

	request
	• Check the transaction based rules are applicable (discounts/tax/ rebates etc.)
	• Verify that the correct code is generated for approved, hold or declined transactions
Negative Scenarios	• Test system with expired card details
	• Test with invalid PIN for credit card
	• Check the inventory by entering wrong code for the item
	• Check how system responds while entering wrong invoice number
	• Test for negative transaction
	• Test the responds of system while entering invalid date for promotional offers on line items
Managing Promotions and Discounts	• Test system for various discount like veteran discount, seasonal discount, undergage or overgage discount etc.
	• Test system for various promotional offers on certain line items
	• Test alert system that notifies end or beginning of seasonal offers
	• Test whether receipt print the exact discount or offers that is leveraged
	• Test system for allocating wrong offers or discount on line item
	• Test the order management process
	• Verify product data obtained after scanning barcode is accurate
Tracking customer's data	• Test for system response with incorrect customer data input
	• Test system for allowing authorized access to customer's confidential data
	• Test the database for recording customer's buying history like (what they buy, how frequent they buy, etc.)
Security & Regulatory Compliance	• Verifying POS system as per regulatory compliances

- Test alert system that notifies security defenders

- Make sure you can void a payment before posting

- Test user profiles and access levels on the POS Software

- Test database consistency

- Verify specific information about each tender cash, coupon identifier, check number and so on

Report testing

- Testing of trend analysis report

- Test information related to credit card transaction should be reflected in reports

- Test for individual as well as consolidated reports of customers buying history

- Test for online report generation

Security Testing for Retail POS Systems

Some recent studies have Point of Sale Systems very high security vulnerabilities. Following measures will help with security of POS

- Security testing in compliance with PCI standard is very crucial to be addressed as the part of enterprise testing

- Actively manage all software on the network so that only authorized software can only execute and installed

- Conduct regular penetration testing to identify attack vectors and vulnerabilities

- Include tests for the presence of unprotected system information and artifacts that would be useful to hackers

- Use vulnerability testing tools

- Create a test bed that imitate a production environment for specific penetration tests and attacks against elements that are not tested in production

Challenges in POS testing

- Multiple Configurations

- Complex interfaces

- Peripheral issues

- Upgrades

- PCI compliance
- Test lab maintenance

Summary

- Retail POS demands high level of testing keeping in mind that its performance and correct functioning directly affect business revenues.

- To reduce the risk and chances of POS failure during transaction process, testing under extreme condition is essential.

- Testing needs to performed at Application as well as Enterprise Level

- Your Testing should cover the following scenarios - Cashier activity, Payment Gateway Processing, Sales, Return & Exchange scenarios, Performance, Negative Scenarios, Managing Promotions and Discounts, Security & Regulatory Compliance.

- Multiple configuration settings, peripheral issues, upgrades are few issues you will need to tide over while testing.

Telecom Domain Testing

Since the shift of telecom sector to computer network and digital medium, telecommunication sector has undergone a major software transformation. Telecom started depending on the various types of software components to deliver many services like routing and switching, VoIP broadband access, etc. Hence, that telecom testing has become an inevitable process.

What is Domain in Testing?

Domain is nothing but the industry for which the software testing project is created. When we talk about software project or development, this term is often referred. For example, Insurance domain, Banking domain, Retail Domain, Telecom Domain, etc.

Usually while developing any specific domain project, domain expert help is sought out. Domain expert are master of the subject and he may know the inside-out of the product or application.

Why Testing Domain Knowledge Matters?

Domain knowledge is quintessential for testing any software product, and it has its own benefits like

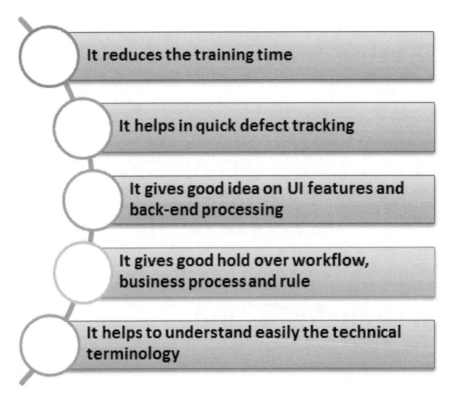

It reduces the training time

It helps in quick defect tracking

It gives good idea on UI features and back-end processing

It gives good hold over workflow, business process and rule

It helps to understand easily the technical terminology

Business Processes in Telecom Industry

For telecom testing end-to-end service verification is important. To ensure efficient testing a good understanding of different Business process is a must.

You need to understand each stage of service deliverability before drafting the test cases.

Telecom services are either based on a business support system that includes IVR's, Call Centers, generating invoices, etc. or an operation support system that includes routers, switches, cell towers, etc.

The following table shows what activities are performed at different levels

Telecom Department	Telecom Activities
Pre-sales	• It handles all the sales information like discounts, services, promos, etc.
Ordering	• Applying for a new connection or disconnecting a connection

Provisioning	• This division deals with the physical connection between customers and TSP (Telecom Service Provider)
Billing	• Under this division, all billing work is done
Service Assurance	• In case of any failure, this division corrects the problem
Inventory Systems	• It is the repository of all information
Tracking	• This division tracks the ordering system and the status of an order

Typical Telecom Business Process

Following is a typical business process in the Telecom Industry.

1. • Telecom Service Provider(TSP) approaches customers

2. • Customer generates enquiry

3. • Customer orders a service to TSP

4. • After technical evaluation, implementation of order takes place

5. • Tracking system tracks the order status, if the order implementation stops at any stage, tracks and tries to fix it

6. • After implementation is done, client starts using the service, the billing starts

7. • Now to support the customer service, service assurance team works

8. • Software will have applications to support each of these

Types of Protocols used in Telecom Industry

Here the popular protocols used in the Telecom industry

- **VoIP technologies**: VoIP, IMS, MPLS, ISDN, PSTN

- **Signaling and Protocols**: SIP, ISDN, Codecs, H.323

- **Wireless technologies:** GPRS, CDMA, GSM, UMTS

- **Network Management:** SNMP

- **Layer 2 Protocols:** ARP, STP, L2TP, PPP

- **Layer 3 protocols/routing:** ICMP, BGP, ISIS, MPLS

- **Infrastructure/Security:** ATM, TCP/IP, LAN/VLAN, SSH

You can learn more about Protocol Testing here

Testing LifeCycle in the Telecom Industry

The Test Lifecycle in the telecom industry is similar to that of any other industry but with a stress on details. Here is how the test lifecycle looks like along with the test artifacts.

Telecom Testing Stage	Test artifacts
• Business View	• Requirement based test artifacts • Feasibility based artifacts • Standard and policy identification based test artifacts • Operation and maintenance considerations related test artifacts
• System/ Architecture	• System test artifacts (Security, Installation) • Test artifacts for virtual prototype • Special system testing artifacts (interoperability, disaster recovery)
• Implementation	• Unit test artifacts • Integration test artifacts • Quality and performance artifacts • Regression, load testing, sanity, etc.
• Deployment	• Acceptance test artifacts

- Integration test artifacts

- Quality and performance artifacts

- Functional test artifacts

- Alpha/Beta test artifacts

Types of Testing Performed on Telecom Software

- Interconnection Testing

- Conformance Testing

- IVR Testing

- Performance Testing

- Security Testing

- Interoperability Testing

- Protocol Testing

- Functional Testing

- Automation Testing

Sample TestCases for Telecom Testing

In Telecom Testing, one must consider testing following

Various Telecom Testing	Testing activities in Telecom
Billing System	<ul><li>Verify, the telephone number of the customer, is registered under telecom operator</li><li>Verify whether number is still working</li><li>Verify the number entered is valid, and it is 10 digit number</li><li>Verify the number is not blocked due to some reasons</li><li>Verify if the number has any outstanding bills, if exist, display it on screen</li><li>Verify the number has all previous accounts or</li></ul>

bills cleared

- Verify the system enables statement generation as per customer requirement

- Verify the system has recorded number of calls accurately

- Verify the plan chosen by the customer displays on the billing system

- Verify the total amount billed is accurate and mapped to the service offered

Application Testing	<ul><li>Protocols, signaling, field testing for IOT</li><li>Usage and functional testing for core **Mobile** handset applications like call, SMS, transfer/hold, etc.</li><li>Testing of various applications like finance, sports and location based services, etc. OSS-BSS testing</li></ul>
OSS-BSS Testing	<ul><li>Billing, customer case, interconnect billing, order and fraud management, revenue assurance</li><li>Network management, mediation, provisioning, etc.</li><li>EAI, CRM & ERP, data warehousing, etc.</li></ul>
Conformance Testing	<ul><li>Electrical interface compatibility</li><li>Conformance of protocol</li><li>Conformance of transport layers</li></ul>
IVR Testing	<ul><li>Interactive test scenarios</li><li>Detection of voice energy</li><li>Broadband audio tones</li><li>Extensive conditional branching sequences</li><li>DTMF Entries</li></ul>

Summary

The telecom service is a very broad field consists of various component including cables, networks, signals, protocols, etc. and their testing requires broad range of testing techniques, so the choice of testing techniques and strategy highly depends on what component of telecom is tested.

The test requirement, scope, test scenarios, testing techniques, testing tools, etc. varies with the type of testing involves, it can be protocol testing for VoIP or wireless device testing for CDMA. The tutorial gives basic but complete overview of how telecom testing can be performed and discuss various prospects that are crucial for telecom testing.